The Spiritual World of Ancient Israel and Greece

Biblical Background to the Novels
Judah Maccabee - Parts 1 & 2

By Brian Godawa

The Spiritual World of Ancient Israel and Greece: Biblical Background to the Novels Judah Maccabee - Parts 1 & 2
1st Edition

Warrior Poet Publishing
www.warriorpoetpublishing.com

ISBN: 978-1-963000-68-9 (paperback)
ISBN: 978-1-963000-69-6 (ebook)
ISBN: 978-1-963000-70-2 (Large Print)

Scripture quotations taken from The Holy Bible: English Standard Version. Wheaton: Standard Bible Society, 2001, unless otherwise indicated in the verse citation.

Other Bible versions cited:
NRSV: The Holy Bible: New Revised Standard Version (Thomas Nelson Publishers, 1989).

LES: Rick Brannan et al., eds., The Lexham English Septuagint (Lexham Press, 2012).

NASB95: New American Standard Bible, 1995 Edition: Paragraph Version (La Habra, CA: The Lockman Foundation, 1995).

Get the novel set *Judah Maccabee: Parts 1 & 2* based on the biblical research of this book you are reading.

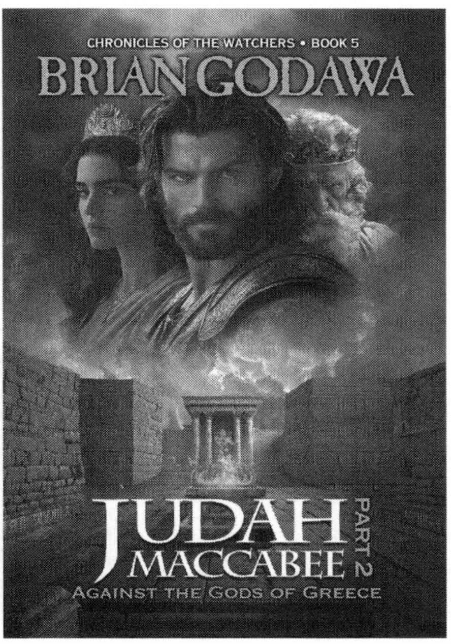

The Supernatural Story of Hanukkah and the Abomination of Desolation.

An epic action Bible novel about the most important Jewish story between the Old and New Testaments, the story of the Maccabees. Respected Christian author Brian Godawa reveals the spiritual realm like never before in this biblically faithful spiritual warfare novel.

https://godawa.com/get-judah-part-1/
(*affiliate link*)

Table of Contents

The links in this book are my Amazon affiliate links.

Chapter 1
The Maccabees and the Bible

The Septuagint

When I decided to write a novel about the Maccabees for this Chronicles series, I knew I would have to explain some things to readers who believe the Bible to be God's written Word as I do. This is because even though the story of the Maccabees is about events in ancient Jewish history, they are not events recorded in the Bible. To be more accurate, they are not in *some* Bibles but are in others. Some Bibles, like the King James Version (KJV) before 1666, the Revised Standard Version (RSV) after 1957, Roman Catholic, and Eastern Orthodox Bibles have several books of Maccabees in them, along with other books, often called Apocrypha, which means "hidden things." The idea there is that early church authorities hid these books because of their questionable authenticity.

But there is some nuance to those inclusions that require explanation. Some traditions (Eastern Orthodox, Syriac) consider the Apocrypha, including Maccabees, to be sacred Scripture, while others (Roman Catholic and the translators of the KJV and RSV) consider them to be helpful and edifying, though not canonical Scripture.

I want to explain some of this nuance by giving a little background on the origin and nature of the Apocrypha and the books of Maccabees without boring the reader with a lengthy academic dissertation, so bear with me. I think it is rewarding.

Before I focus in on the actual books of the Maccabees, I want to start with their origin in a broader manuscript tradition called the Septuagint. The Septuagint broadly refers to ancient Greek translations of the Hebrew scriptures, to which Christians refer as the Old Testament. The term *Septuagint*, also called The Translation of the

Seventy, is derived from the Latin word *septuaginta*, meaning "seventy." It comes from a Jewish legend recorded in an apocryphal manuscript titled *The Letter of Aristeas*, which claims that 72 Jewish scholars, six from each of the twelve tribes of Israel, translated the first five books of Moses—the Torah, or Pentateuch—into Greek in Alexandria, Egypt, around 250 BC. The term Septuagint simply rounds down 72 to 70 and, therefore, is often referred to by LXX, its Roman numerical equivalent.

The legend was rooted in the historical fact of Greece's imperial cultural dominance caused by Alexander the Great's conquest of the known world by the time of his death in 323 BC. His surviving empire was divided between four of his generals, whose reigns competed for the next couple of centuries until Rome rose to dominance. The "Greekification" of everything became known as Hellenism—even today, Greece's official name is the Hellenic Republic—and it influenced everyone's lives economically, culturally and linguistically. The Greek language became the *lingua franca* of the empire, the common language everyone spoke to be able to interact between their various ethnicities and languages.

Though the Hebrews kept their own language and ethnic culture, they adopted the Greek language and some of the culture as well. As the legend goes, around 250 BC, the Greek Pharaoh in Egypt, Ptolemy II Philadelphus, commissioned 72 Jewish scribes to come to Alexandria from Jerusalem to translate the Hebrew scriptures for his own library. They did so for the first five books of the Law (Torah). Over the following decades, Jewish translators translated into Greek the other two "parts" of the Hebrew Bible, the Prophets and the Writings.

This is of significance for the Christian reader because many mistakenly believe that the Hebrew text that we currently have of the Old Testament is always the most accurate representation of the original text. After all, the original writings were in Hebrew, not Greek, right?

Actually, the oldest Hebrew manuscripts of the Old Testament that we had until the discovery of the Dead Sea Scrolls (1946-1956), were from the Middle Ages of the 10th and 11th centuries AD. These handwritten manuscripts were based on what is today called the Masoretic Text (MT), a textual tradition whose name derives from the Masoretes, a community of Jewish scribes who standardized the text of the Hebrew scriptures and copied and distributed them between the 7th and 10th centuries AD. With the scrolls uncovered from the Dead Sea caves of Qumran, we discovered Greek and Hebrew texts that were as much as a thousand years older than the earliest known Hebrew manuscripts at the time. And scholarship soon discovered that these earlier manuscripts sometimes correlated with the Septuagint and sometimes with the Masoretic Text. This means that sometimes the Greek translation of the Old Testament was based on an older, and possibly more accurate, Hebrew manuscript tradition than the MT.[1]

Here's where a historical twist comes in that makes the story fascinating. By the time of Christ, during the second Temple period, the Jewish community accepted the Greek translations of the Old Testament texts as inspired by God. But it was not just the scribes, Pharisees, and Sadducees who did so. Both Jesus and the Apostles who wrote the New Testament, more often than not, quoted from the Greek translation (not the Hebrew text) as God's Word![2]

This is significant for the Christian, because it establishes that the Hebrew MT is not always the best or most original language upon which we can rely. And the LXX was therefore based on an older, and

---

[1] Karen H. Jobes and Moisés Silva, *Invitation to the Septuagint,* (Grand Rapids, MI, Baker Academic, 2000), 167-182.

[2] Scholars have itemized all the Old Testament quotations and allusions. Moises Silva and Karen Jobes explain that most of the scriptural quotations in the Gospels and Acts follow the LXX, a few follow the MT, and others don't match up with either. Richard Longenecker chronicles that in the letters of Paul in particular, "of the approximately one hundred Old Testament passages quoted by Paul in his letters (disengaging the conflated texts and the possible dual sources, and treating each separately), over half are either absolute or virtual reproductions of the LXX, with almost half of these at variance with the MT. On the other hand, four are in agreement with the MT against the LXX (Job 41:11; 5:13; Ps 112:9; Num 16:5), and approximately forty vary from both the LXX and the MT to a greater or lesser degree." Richard N. Longenecker, *Biblical Exegesis in the Apostolic Period, 2nd ed.* (Grand Rapids, MI; Vancouver: W. B. Eerdmans; Regent College Pub., 1999), 96–97.

sometimes different, Hebrew text. The modern bias toward the MT as more "original" than the LXX text is then unfounded.

As it turns out, the MT has many significant theological problems that we cannot ignore because they affect biblical theology. A well-known case is the messianic prophecy of Isaiah 7:14, "Therefore the Lord himself will give you a sign. Behold, the virgin shall conceive and bear a son, and shall call his name Immanuel."

The word for "virgin" in the Hebrew MT is *almah*, which does not mean virgin, but simply young maiden. Whereas, in the Greek LXX, the word for "virgin" is *parthenos*, which assuredly means *virgin*. The Gospel of Matthew quotes from the Greek text (Matthew 1:23) to validate the claim that a virgin gave birth to Jesus. As much as one wants to say that a young maiden *could* be a virgin, it is not intrinsic to the Hebrew word. So the Apostle Matthew considered the Greek translation as *virgin* as God's inspired Word. Not so much to modern Jews who seek to deny Jesus's Messiahship.

Another example of theological variation in the MT can be found in the translation of Deuteronomy 32:43. The LXX renders it,

> Delight, O heavens, with him
>   and worship him, you sons of God.
> Delight, O nations, with his people
>   and prevail with him, all you angels of God.[3]

The MT simply translates that verse as, "O nations, rejoice His people." That's it. Nothing else. It ignores the spiritual "heavens" and only mentions the natural "nations." It also completely cuts out the references to the divine sons of God, a clear example of the anti-Christian bias of Jewish scribes trying to delete the plurality of divinity in the text.

Interestingly, a Dead Sea Scroll fragment of this text, much older than the MT, confirms the LXX's supernatural flavor,

---

[3] Rick Brannan et al., eds., *The Lexham English Septuagint* (Bellingham, WA: Lexham Press, 2012), Dt 32:43.

O heavens, rejoice with Him
Bow to Him, all gods.[4]

In fact, the Jewish community standardized the MT's text to distinguish its translation of the Hebrew Scriptures from that of the Greek version adopted by the Church, despite the fact that Second Temple Jews before them, as well as the first Christians that formed part of that Jewish community, had accepted the LXX as inspired! With the destruction of Israel and the temple in AD 70, Christianity successfully outgrew Judaism and overshadowed its Old Covenant origins. Anti-Christian Jews did not want the same Bible as their enemies.[5]

I use these two cases out of many to prove that Christian apologists are not being truthful when they argue that the translational differences of the Old Testament are negligible and do not really affect theological content. That is simply not true. There are entire books itemizing the many significant theological translational differences between the LXX and the MT, as well as variations within those traditions.[6] This is not to disparage the MT or to always prioritize the LXX over it. And it does not discredit the Old Testament's authority. My point is that the LXX translation has a distinguished authoritative tradition used by Jesus (as quoted in the four gospels), the Apostles, and the early Church. So we must afford it due respect.

And if that is the case, then what do we make of the fact that the apocryphal books of the Maccabees are part of the Greek translation of the Hebrew Scriptures quoted by Jesus and the Apostles as God's written Word?

---

4 Jeffrey H. Tigay, *Deuteronomy, The JPS Torah Commentary*, 516 (Philadelphia: Jewish Publication Society, 1996), 314

5 Roger T. Beckwith, *The Old Testament Canon of the New Testament Church and Its Background in Early Judaism* (London: SPCK, 1985), 382.

6 Emanuel Tov, *Textual Criticism of the Hebrew Bible, Second Revised Edition* (Minneapolis: Fortress Press, 1992, 2001); Timothy Michael Law, *When God Spoke Greek: The Septuagint and the Making of the Christian Bible* (New York: Oxford University Press, 2013).

The Apocrypha

I'm sorry to complicate things a bit more, but that previous claim I just made above is what many people think, but it's not entirely true. We are not sure that the books that are in our modern versions of the LXX were actually in the Greek corpus that Jesus and the Apostles quoted. The reason is that our modern versions of the LXX are collections of books *into one volume* that goes back only to about the second century AD at most. Before that time, and during the time of Jesus and the Apostles, there was no codified single book called "the Septuagint" that included specific books beyond the first five books of Moses. When Jesus and the Apostles quoted from the Greek Old Testament, they were quoting from Greek scrolls, but we do not have those scrolls and they were not collected into a single book called "the Septuagint."

In fact, the very ancient form of the book with which we are familiar is called a *codex*, pages bound between two covers. It wasn't until the second century that Christians preferred the easily transportable and referenceable codex for the purpose of gathering sacred writings together into single volumes. The oldest manuscript we currently have of a single-volume Greek translation of the Old Testament that includes the Apocrypha is Codex Vaticanus, dated to the 4th century AD.

Nevertheless, what we call the Septuagint was compiled by the first Christians based on beliefs about which texts were God's written Word to man and not merely spiritually edifying. This is where the word *canon* comes in. The biblical canon is defined as the list of books Christians consider authoritative as God's written Word. Now, the biblical canon also has a long history of scholarly debate that goes beyond the scope of this little book. But it suffices to say that it took several centuries to solidify that biblical canon within the Christian Church. Part of the questioning involved the very books in the LXX that some Jews or Christians accepted as authoritative while others did not.

So what books are in the Septuagint? The oldest full manuscript we have, called Vaticanus, contains the thirty-nine books of the Old Testament from Genesis to Malachi (with some variations of nomenclature and order), but also includes the apocryphal books of Wisdom of Solomon, Ecclesiasticus (or Wisdom of Ben Sirach), Judith, Tobit, Baruch, Susanna, Bel and the Dragon, and the Epistle of Jeremiah. The careful reader will notice that the books of the Maccabees are not in this list of added texts.

Vaticanus may be the oldest full manuscript of the Septuagint we have, but it is not the only one, and the oldest does not always mean the most accurate, if it is based on lesser quality copies. These are things scholar fuss over, but the short of it is that we have two other significant codexes of the Septuagint, Sinaiticus (also 4th century) and Alexandrinus (5th century), which have other apocryphal books included in their texts, such as the Odes of Solomon, the Prayer of Manasseh, and the four individual books of 1-4 Maccabees, the latter of which serve as the foundation of my novels, *Judah Maccabee: Part 1* and *Part 2*.

So the books of the Maccabees were part of the Greek texts over which Christians debated in the first centuries of the canonization process, with reputable Church fathers and scholars on both sides of the debate. Clement of Rome, Irenaeus, Tertullian, Cyprian, Clement of Alexandria, and Origen were just some of those most respected who considered at least some of the Apocrypha to be inspired Scripture. But as Francis Beckwith concludes, support for the Apocrypha's canonicity was not monolithic: "All that was agreed was that the Apocrypha were to be read and esteemed, not that they were to be treated as Scripture."[7]

---

[7] Roger T. Beckwith, *The Old Testament Canon of the New Testament Church and Its Background in Early Judaism* (London: SPCK, 1985), 386, 394. One of the strongest arguments for the Apocrypha not being considered canonical is that Jesus and the Apostles never quoted from those books as Scripture. But this is not an absolute proof, because there are nine other Old Testament books never quoted in the New Testament as well: Judges, Ruth, Ezra, Esther, Ecclesiastes, Song of Solomon, Lamentations, Obadiah, and Zephaniah. Obadiah and Zephaniah, however, were considered a part of the singular category called "The Twelve" in reference to the twelve minor prophets, so they may be assumed under that category. And it must be remembered that the New Testament also quotes from many sources that are *not* considered canonical but nevertheless considered relevant or truthful.

Later, Martin Luther expressed a common Reformed position when he described the Apocrypha as "books which are not to be equated with Holy Scripture and yet which are useful and good to read."[8]

Bible scholar John Bartlett adds,

> In England the Calvinist-inspired Geneva Bible (1560) included the apocryphal books, accepting them 'for their knowledge of history and instruction of godly manners', a phrase taken up in the Church of England's Thirty-Nine Articles of Religion, which state that 'the other [i.e. apocryphal] books…the Church doth read for example of life and instruction of manners; but yet doth it not apply them to establish any doctrine'.[9]

In a sense, this standard still holds today. Even though Protestants may not agree with the Roman Catholic or Eastern Orthodox views of the Apocrypha as canonical or deuterocanonical, scholarship maintains they are nevertheless worthy of respect to be studied and afforded esteem for basic historical purposes. And that is the position that I took as author of the *Judah Maccabee* novels. God is sovereignly involved in all history, not only in biblically canonical history.

So let's take a closer look at these books of 1-4 Maccabees to see what we can learn from them as part of God's redemptive narrative (His-story).

Books of the Maccabees

Though the books of the Maccabees are not included in the Hebrew canon, Jews annually celebrate certain narrative events in 1 and 2 Maccabees to this day in the holiday of Hanukkah, a festival the Bible does not explicitly command.

---

8 Thomas Fischer, "Maccabees, Books of: First and Second Maccabees," in *The Anchor Yale Bible Dictionary*, ed. David Noel Freedman, trans. Frederick Cryer (New York: Doubleday, 1992), 439.

9 John R. Bartlett, *1 Maccabees, Guides to Apocrypha and Pseudepigrapha* (Sheffield, England: Sheffield Academic Press, 1998), 14.

Though our extant manuscripts of the Maccabees books are in Greek, most scholars believe that 1 Maccabees was translated from an original Hebrew text.

Here are what the four books are about:

1 Maccabees. This book describes Jewish efforts to withstand the oppression of the Hellenistic Seleucid empire against their ethnic identity during the period of c. 175-134 BC. It describes the actions of king Antiochus IV Epiphanes and others against the Jews and the wars spawned when the sons of Mattathias ben Johannan rose to defend Israel. Scholars consider the books as propaganda for the Hasmonean dynasty of priests that would lead up to the Pharisees of Jesus' day.

My *Judah Maccabee* novels cover this main narrative surrounding the Maccabean revolt against Antiochus and ends with the recovery and cleansing of the temple in Jerusalem in 164 BC. Though the battles between the Jews and the Seleucids were far from over after that event, it nevertheless marked a significant victory and historical turning point that resulted in the commemoration of the Jewish holiday of Hanukkah mentioned above. Many scholars also believe 1 Maccabees may very well reflect Sadducean theology because it avoids any description of spiritual warfare or resurrection.

2 Maccabees. This book covers the similar time period and events as 1 Maccabees of the Jews under Seleucid rule but ends with the fall of the Seleucid empire in 161 BC. It is considered a stark, contrasting view from 1 Maccabees because it charges Israel with spiritual guilt for disobedience to God resulting in heaven's punishment of Israel. If 1 Maccabees is pro-Hasmonean and Sadducean, many scholars consider 2 Maccabees anti-Hasmonean and Pharisaic because it affirms spiritual warfare of angels as well as personal bodily resurrection.

3 Maccabees. This book deals with similar themes as 2 Maccabees but addresses Jews in Egypt under Ptolemy IV fifty years before the events of the Maccabean Revolt of 167 BC.

4 Maccabees. This book is not historical but more of a philosophical treatise about the superiority of reason over emotions, a specifically Hellenistic view. But it gives some narrative expansion to the martyrdom accounts of Jews under Antiochus Epiphanes detailed in 2 Maccabees (e.g., Eleazar, and a woman and her seven sons). Early Christians drew heavily from these reports for encouragement in facing their own martyrdom. My *Judah Maccabee* novels also drew from this book for its martyr stories.

Another source for the novels is the respected first-century Jewish historian Josephus, who used 1 Maccabees and other ancient historical sources to write about the Maccabean Revolt as a primer to the Jewish Revolt against Rome of AD 66-70.[10]

Hanukkah

The eight-day festival tied to the Maccabean revolt is Hanukkah, a word that means "dedication" but is ultimately translated as "Festival of Lights." This is based on a miracle in the days of the Maccabees claimed by Jewish rabbinic legend. The Talmud describes the event as occurring after Judas cleansed the temple from its Greek defilement. While neither the books of Maccabees nor Josephus mention this legend, Jews nevertheless celebrate it to this day.

According to Torah, the priests were to keep lit the holy place's famous lampstand of the Menorah with undefiled oil continuously day and night. But they were only able to find enough oil for one day. They used it anyway, and it miraculously kept the Menorah lit for eight days until they could obtain more holy oil.[11] Hanukkah commemorates that miracle legend.

---

[10] Josephus, *Jewish Antiquities*, 12.5 - 13.7

[11] Babylonian Talmud, *Tractate Shabbat* 21b.10 https://www.sefaria.org/Shabbat.21b.10?lang=bi&with=all&lang2=en

Maccabees and Daniel

A significant character in the Judah Maccabee novels is a 90-year-old Hebrew scribe named Eleazar, a historical character whom Antiochus martyred for his faith.[12] He also became a literary source within the story for explaining Daniel's prophecies and applying them to contemporary events of their day. Although the writers of Maccabees did not explicitly claim fulfillment of Bible prophecy, several implicit references, including the term "abomination of desolation" point to knowledge of the book of Daniel. Some early Church fathers considered the first two books of Maccabees as chronicling events prophesied by Daniel, from the rise of Alexander the Great to Antiochus Epiphanes and the subsequent reign of Gentile powers over Israel until the coming of the Messiah.[13]

Here is a chart of possible fulfillments of the Maccabean events in Daniel's prophecies:[14]

Daniel Citation	Text or Symbols	Fulfillment
8:5-8, 21-22	Male goat and great horn	Alexander the Great
8:8, 22	Four horns from the broken great horn	The four kings that split up the empire after Alexander's death: Ptolemy (Egypt), Seleucus (Persia), Antigonis (Asia Minor), and Cassander (Macedon)
8:9, 23-26	Little horn grows exceedingly great toward the glorious land	Antiochus IV Epiphanes (Seleucid) turns his attention to Jerusalem

12 2 Maccabees 6:18-31; 4 Maccabees 5:1-6:35.

13 Bartlett lists among the Church fathers to make this connection: Clement of Alexandria, Hippolytus, Tertullian, Origen, Cyprian, Eusebius of Caesarea. John R. Bartlett, *1 Maccabees, Guides to Apocrypha and Pseudepigrapha* (Sheffield, England: Sheffield Academic Press, 1998), 16.

14 I have drawn much of the information in this chart from: Jay Rogers, *In the Days of These Kings: The Book of Daniel in Preterist Perspective* (Clermont, FL: Media House International, 2017), Philip Mauro, *The Seventy Weeks and the Great Tribulation: A Study of the Last Two Visions of Daniel, and of the Olivet Discourse of the Lord Jesus Christ* (Public Domain, 1921, 1944), and Bruce Gore's teaching "Antiochus Epiphanes and the Maccabees," https://www.youtube.com/watch?v=6hwkThHYBXs

8:11-12	Burnt offering and sanctuary overthrown	Antiochus IV defiling the temple with a statue of Zeus and pig offering
11:3-4	A mighty king to arise	Alexander the Great
11:4	Kingdom divided to the four winds of heaven	The four kings that split up the empire after Alexander's death
Chapter 11	King of the South	Ptolemaic kings of Egypt
Chapter 11	King of the North	Seleucid kings of Syria/Babylon
11:5-6	North-South alliance	First Syrian War: Ptolemy II of Egypt vs. Antiochus I of Seleucia; Antiochus II marries Ptolemy's daughter Berenice in alliance
11:7-9	A branch arises in the South and attacks the fortress of the North	Ptolemy III arises when his sister Berenice is murdered and makes war on Seleucus II of Syria; Ptolemy occupies Antioch in Syria
11:10-12	Sons of the King of the North wage war on the King of the South	Fourth Syrian War: Sons of Seleucus, Seleucus III Soter and Antiochus III the Great, attack Ptolemy IV Philopater of Egypt
11:13-18	The King of the North raises a multitude	Fifth Syrian War: Ptolemy IV dies and Antiochus III attacks Syria to regain; includes either the battle of Panium or battle of Sidon
11:17-19	"shall give him the daughter"	Antiochus III gives his daughter Cleopatra I to Ptolemy V in a peace treaty
11:21	"And in his place a despicable person will arise on whom they have not conferred the majesty of the kingdom, and he will come in without warning and he will seize the kingdom by deceit."	175 BC; Antiochus IV is the despicable one who was not next in line for kingship; he claims to rule on behalf of Demetrius, the heir, while Demetrius is in Rome as hostage
11:23	"After an alliance is made with him he will practice deception, and he will go up and gain power with a small force of people."	After Antiochus IV gets his small military force in place, he disavows Demetrius as heir and takes the throne for himself

11:22	"The overflowing forces will be flooded away before him and shattered, and also the prince of the covenant."	Sixth Syrian War: Antiochus IV comes to power and attacks both the Jews and Ptolemy VI of Egypt; the prince of the covenant may be the righteous high priest Onias III
11:24	"In a time of tranquility he will enter the richest parts of the realm, and he will accomplish what his fathers never did, nor his ancestors; he will distribute plunder, booty and possessions among them, and he will devise his schemes against strongholds, but only for a time."	Antiochus IV uses his wealth to buy loyalty in the Syrian provinces; he plunders temples, including the temple in Jerusalem, and plans a campaign against Egypt in the South; through the new high priest Jason, Antiochus Hellenizes Jerusalem, leading to the Maccabean Revolt
11:25-26	"He will stir up his strength and courage against the king of the South with a large army; so the king of the South will mobilize an extremely large and mighty army for war; but he will not stand, for schemes will be devised against him. Those who eat his choice food will destroy him, and his army will overflow, but many will fall down slain."	170 BC; Antiochus IV angers the King of the South, Ptolemy VI, and sends his army toward Syria, but Antiochus ambushes the Egyptian forces at Pelusium and takes much of Egypt, except for Alexandria; Ptolemy becomes his puppet king
11:27	"As for both kings, their hearts will be intent on evil, and they will speak lies to each other at the same table; but it will not succeed, for the end is still to come at the appointed time."	Two Ptolemys now rule Egypt together: Ptolemy VIII governs Alexandria while Ptolemy VI governs the rest of Egypt
11:28	"Then he will return to his land with much plunder; but his heart will be set against the holy covenant, and he will take action and then return to his own land."	169 BC; Antiochus IV leaves Egypt and returns to Syria with his Egyptian plunder; he stops at Jerusalem and sacks it for gold and silver
11:29-30	"At the appointed time he will return and come into the South, but this last time it will not turn out the way it did before. For ships of Kittim will come against him; therefore he will be disheartened and will return and become enraged at the holy covenant and take action; so he will come back	168 BC; Antiochus IV returns to invade Egypt a second time and take Alexandria but Rome stops him ("Kittim") Antiochus returns to Syria but again becomes enraged at a civil war that has begun in Jerusalem, prompting him to attack Jerusalem

	and show regard for those who forsake the holy covenant."	
11:31	"Forces from him will arise, desecrate the sanctuary fortress, and do away with the regular sacrifice. And they will set up the abomination of desolation."	167 BC; Antiochus IV halts the daily sacrifices and sacrifices a pig to Zeus on the altar; forces the Jews to forsake their covenant obedience by eating swine and not observing circumcision, dietary laws, or the Sabbath
11:32-35	"By smooth words he will turn to godlessness those who act wickedly toward the covenant, but the people who know their God will display strength and take action…Some of those who have insight will fall, in order to refine, purge and make them pure until the end time; because it is still to come at the appointed time."	Hellenist Jews are seduced to give up their obedience to the Mosaic covenant. But… 165 BC; the Maccabean Revolt against Antiochus IV results in many martyrs; the Maccabees successfully force the Seleucids out of Jerusalem, cleanse the temple, and resumes the Mosaic sacrifices
11:36-45	The Willful King who exalts himself against God and also enters glorious land rules at the time of the end	1st Century BC. Probable options: Herod the Great, Julius Caesar and the line of Caesars, Titus or Antiochus IV. Antiochus the IV is the least likely.

The Absence of Prophets

In the *Judah Maccabee* novels, I refer to the fact that prophecy had ceased in Israel with the death of its last prophet, Malachi, around 400 BC, over two hundred years before the Maccabean Revolt.

Since only prophets could speak for Yahweh and the only ones whose writings could be considered authoritative Scripture, this cessation of prophecy refers to the closing of the Old Testament canon. But this truth's implications are profound. Why would Yahweh cease to speak to his people? And for how long would he remain silent?

Modern liberal/critical scholarship tries to discredit the Old Testament by arguing that there was never any fixed Old Testament canon, that there was just a chaotic collection of different versions of manuscripts that some Jews accepted and other Jews did not, and that the Jewish religion was always evolving. This view fails to take into account that, long before Jesus's time, there had already been an accepted canon of Scripture consisting of the Law, the Prophets, and the Writings. Jesus himself had referred to them as such.[15]

First-century AD Jewish scholar Josephus affirmed the Old Testament's tripartite division.[16] And second-century AD Jewish scholarship also confirmed that the Holy Spirit ceased speaking to God's people:

> "When the latter prophets died, that is, Haggai, Zechariah, and Malachi, then the Holy Spirit came to an end in Israel. But even then they made them hear through an echo" (*t. Soṭah* 13:3 A, B).[17]

But even at the time of the Maccabees in 167 BC, Jews believed prophecy had ceased in Israel.

> 1 Maccabees 9:27 (LES)
> And there was great distress in Israel, such that had never happened from that time when the prophet had ceased from being seen among them.[18]

What about the Old Testament itself? Does it explicitly say that prophecy had ceased? Maybe not using those words, but it certainly implied it with Malachi's final words.

> Malachi 4:5–6
> "Behold, I will send you Elijah the prophet before the great and awesome day of the LORD comes."

As Jesus explained, John the Baptizer was the spiritual or figurative Elijah who fulfilled Malachi's prediction (Matthew 11:14; Mark 9:11-13; Luke 1:16-17). So, why is this cessation important?

---

[15] Matthew 7:12; 22:40; Luke 24:44.

[16] *Against Apion* 1.38-42. Flavius Josephus, *The Works of Josephus: Complete and Unabridged*, ed. William Whiston (Peabody, MA: Hendrickson, 1987), 776.

[17] S. G. Dempster, "Canon, Canonization," in *Dictionary of the Old Testament: Prophets*, eds. Mark J. Boda and Gordon J. McConville (Downers Grove, IL; Nottingham, England: IVP Academic; InterVarsity Press, 2012), 74.

[18] See also 1 Maccabees 4:46 and 14:41.

The idea was that Israel's serial apostasy from Yahweh throughout her entire history had made her so incorrigible that God would cease talking to her as a people until he would send the final herald of Messiah and judgment, Elijah (that is, John the Baptizer). Elijah then announced the final prophet of Israel, Messiah, to be the Father's final spokesman, with the final offer of a New Covenant in the last days of the Old Covenant.

> Hebrews 1:1–2
> Long ago, at many times and in many ways, God spoke to our fathers by the prophets, but in these last days he has spoken to us by his Son.

> Luke 16:16
> [Jesus:] "The Law and the Prophets were until John [the Baptizer]; since then the good news of the kingdom of God is preached.

So, Yahweh had remained silent toward Israel for about four hundred years until he sent Messiah.

But there is a corollary to this lack of God's spirit. It was the lack of his presence in his own house in Israel's midst.

The Absence of God from the Temple

The temple in Jerusalem had been Yahweh's "house" for about four hundred years after Solomon built it. Yahweh's presence followed the holy Ark of the Covenant that he had placed inside the temple's Holy of Holies. Thus, the temple represented God's dwelling with his people as it also housed his Shekinah glory cloud (Exodus 40:34-35).

But because of Israel's continuous apostasy, the prophet Ezekiel explained that God himself would remove his presence from that temple. The absence of God's presence would make both the temple and the city of Jerusalem "unholy" and prepared for judgment.

That judgment occurred in 586 BC when King Nebuchadnezzar's Babylonian armies destroyed the temple and city and the Ark of the

Covenant was lost forever to history, conspiracy theories notwithstanding.

Ezekiel's vision described the supernatural throne guardians, the cherubim, as rising up to the threshold of the temple *and leaving*…

> Ezekiel 10:18–19
> Then the glory of the LORD went out from the threshold of the house and stood over the cherubim. And the cherubim lifted up their wings and mounted up from the earth before my eyes as they went out.

God's holy presence, his "glory," left Israel's midst just prior to the Babylonian Exile in 586 BC. Around 400 BC, God stopped speaking to Israel through his prophets until he would return to Zion in the incarnate form of Messiah to bring salvation from their idolatry against Yahweh.

> Zechariah 8:3, 9:9
> Thus says the LORD: I will return to Zion and will dwell in the midst of Jerusalem. … Rejoice greatly, O daughter of Zion! Shout aloud, O daughter of Jerusalem! Behold, your king is coming to you; righteous and having salvation is he, humble and mounted on a donkey, on a colt, the foal of a donkey. [fulfilled in Matthew 21:1-11]

The time of the Maccabees was during that 400-year period of God's withdrawn presence and silence toward Israel. But does that mean that God had completely withdrawn his hand from Israel?

The Absence of Angels?

Though God had withdrawn his presence from the Jerusalem temple and his prophetic voice from the people of Israel, he was still involved in the events of the Maccabees because God remains sovereign over all history, regardless of his relational disposition. As Daniel had written, "He changes times and seasons; he removes kings and sets up kings" (Daniel 2:21). Or as Job had confirmed, "The deceived and the deceiver are his. … He makes nations great, and he destroys them; he enlarges nations, and leads them away" (Job 12:16b, 23).

From before time to the end of time and beyond, Scripture proclaims Yahweh works to accomplish his predestined purposes, period. There is no exception.

> Isaiah 46:9–10
> [Yahweh:] "I am God, and there is none like me, declaring the end from the beginning and from ancient times things not yet done, saying, 'My counsel shall stand, and I will accomplish all my purpose.'"

We could perhaps see a parallel between the Intertestamental period of silence and that described in the book of Esther, where God is nowhere mentioned in the story because it appears that God is nowhere to be found. But he is, in fact, orchestrating his purposes behind the scenes even if we don't see his presence.

This is why the *Judah Maccabee* novels continue the supernatural warfare between the Watchers that marks the Chronicles series of books. We may not see what is going on behind the veil of the natural world, but it is surely taking place. The biblical picture is consistently that of a heavenly world of activity tied directly to the earthly world of activity (Judges 5:19-20; Daniel 10:12-21; 1Kings 22:19-23).

Although not Scripture, the second book of Maccabees makes the same claim of spiritual warfare during their battle for freedom from Antiochus Epiphanes and his abominable empire of desolation. The first two of these passages describes the spiritual war depicted in the *Judah Maccabee* novels:

> 2 Maccabees 5:1–4 (LES)
> (*Spirit war over Egypt*)
> Now about this time, Antiochus went on a second departure into Egypt. It happened that throughout the entire city for almost forty days, horsemen having raiment interwoven with gold appeared running through the air and being fully armed

by cohorts with spears and drawn swords. And troops of horses were set in array, and they were making attacks and counter attacks from both sides. And there was a brandishing of shields and an abundance of wrought weapons and flights of arrows and the shining forth of golden ornaments and manifold breastplates.

2 Maccabees 11:6–8 (LES)
(*Judas in his fight against Lysias at Beth-Zur*)
But when those with Maccabeus heard of his besieging the strongholds, they were beseeching together with the multitudes the Lord with lamentations and tears to send a good angel for salvation in Israel. Maccabeus himself first took up his weapons. He urged the others at the same time to make a desperate attempt with him to come to the aid of their kinfolk. And so with one accord they rushed out willingly. And there, while they were near Jerusalem, appeared one going before them on horseback in brilliant raiment brandishing golden weaponry.

2 Maccabees 10:29–31 (LES)
(*Judas in a battle against Timothy after the temple is rededicated*)
Now as the battle became fierce, five illustrious men upon horses with golden bridles appeared from heaven before opposing forces, and two were leading the Judeans. And putting Maccabeus in their midst and sheltering him with their own armor, they were keeping him safe from harm. But they were repeatedly sending arrows and lightning toward the opposing ones on account of which they were divided, being thrown into confusion with blindness and being completely disordered.

The Absence of High Priesthood

Another consequence of this time period of national apostasy in Israel was the legitimate priesthood's elimination. Onias III had become high priest in about 190 BC. As Bruce Gore explains, Onias "was the legitimate high priest, a direct descendant of King David's own high priest, the famous Zadok who had himself descended from Aaron. They called themselves the Hasidim (pious ones), and were a large, popular, and conservative movement" called the Oniads.[19] In the books of the Maccabees, the Hebrew "Hasidim" are translated into Greek as, "Hasideans."

When Antiochus IV Epiphanes became king in 175 BC, Onias's brother Jason sought to steal the high priesthood through deception. Jason was a Hellenist who despised his brother's piety. While on mission to bring taxes to the king on Onias's behalf, Jason bribed Antiochus with an additional hoard of silver and the promise to build a Greek gymnasium in Jerusalem and enroll the people of Jerusalem as citizens of Antioch, the Seleucid capital. King Antiochus, who had little concern for Jewish politics, accepted the deal, which began the Jews' further plunge into apostasy (2 Maccabees 4:7-10).

A Greek gymnasium was a blasphemous offense to devout Jews because it was not merely a location of physical exercise and sport; it was an indoctrination center into Greek philosophy and morality for the youth, also called "ephebes." Its involvement violated the Torah on many levels. The participants would exercise and compete in the nude and engage in pederastic liaisons popular amongst the Greeks. The ephebes would wear a broad-brimmed Greek hat called a *petasos*, another distinguishing mark of Hellenism and like that worn by the Greek god Hermes (2 Maccabees 4:12).

Nakedness also resulted in Jews being conspicuous for their circumcision, which inspired many of them to "undo" their sign of the holy covenant in order to be more accepted as Hellenist.[20] Such undoing was tantamount to a rejection of their covenant with Yahweh.

---

[19] Bruce W. Gore, *Historical and Chronological Context of the Bible* (Trafford Publishing, 2006), 10.16.

[20] The Assumption of Moses 8:3 explains how they might reverse circumcision: "...and their young sons shall be operated on by the physicians in order to bring forward their foreskin." Robert Henry Charles, ed., *Pseudepigrapha of the Old Testament, vol. 2* (Oxford: Clarendon Press, 1913), 420.

As the author of 2 Maccabees explains, this resulted in a Hellenist cultural supremacy that resulted in serious apostasy of the most important ruling class of priests, leading to God's chastisement of all Israel.

> 2 Maccabees 4:14-17 (RSV)
> ...that the priests were no longer intent upon their service at the altar. Despising the sanctuary and neglecting the sacrifices, they hurried to take part in the unlawful proceedings...disdaining the honors prized by their ancestors and putting the highest value upon Greek forms of prestige. For this reason heavy disaster overtook them, and those whose ways of living they admired and wished to imitate completely became their enemies and punished them. It is no light thing to show irreverence to the divine laws—a fact that later events will make clear.

Onias was exiled in Antioch as Jason spent the next three years Hellenizing much of Jerusalem and Judea. But then, in 172 BC, Menelaus, a member of the priestly order of Bilgah, pulled the same trick on Jason that Jason had pulled on Onias: Menelaus visited King Antiochus and out-bribed Jason to win Israel's high priesthood (2 Maccabees 4:23-26).

But there was a problem: according to Torah, Menelaus was not a Zadokite and, therefore, not a legitimate high priest.[21] Not only that, but he is described as "having the hot temper of a cruel tyrant and the rage of a savage wild beast" (2 Maccabees 4:25). Menelaus was so determined to retain his high priesthood that he had Onias, the rightful high priest, assassinated in Daphne outside of Antioch to consolidate his family's new hold on power. Menelaus was a crucial player in many of the narrative's compounding factors, from temple robberies to the civil war to the persecution of the Jews. Antiochus's commander,

---

[21] Uriel Rappaport, "Menelaus (Person)," in *The Anchor Yale Bible Dictionary*, ed. David Noel Freedman (New York: Doubleday, 1992), 694. See also 2 Maccabees 4:25.

Lysias, ended up blaming Menelaus for "all the trouble" they had experienced in the Maccabean Revolt (2 Maccabees 3:4).

With the Maccabean revolution's success, the sons of Mattathias would take over the high priest role and become the founding members of the Hasmonean dynasty ("sons of Hasamonai").[22] So the irony of history is that the very ones who cleansed the temple ended setting up an illegitimate and unbiblical priesthood. The heroes became villains.

Bible scholar Bruce Gore concludes that this appropriation of the office of high priest constituted another component of Israel's apostasy: "In fact from that moment until the fall of Jerusalem in AD 70, no legitimate descendent of Aaron ever served as high priest. From the New Testament point of view, the next and final high priest was Messiah."

So the absence of God's presence in the temple, the absence of his speaking through his prophets, and the absence of legitimate high priests in Israel all added up to portray a picture of God, Israel's husband, pulling away and being silent toward his spiritually estranged wife.

But his sovereign providence would continue behind the scenes until he would send Messiah to save that unfaithful wife from the monster Gentile kingdoms' centuries-long rule. Her rejection of Messiah (except for the Remnant) would result in an ultimate divorce decree, destruction of temple, and establishment of a New Covenant kingdom.[23] But that is a story I have told in another novel series, Chronicles of the Apocalypse.

Resurrection

In the Old Testament, the concept of life after death was of little interest. The ancient Hebrews' focus was on this world rather than the next. As N. T. Wright explains, "The hope of the biblical writers, which was

---

[22] Lester L. Grabbe, "Hasmoneans," in *The New Interpreter's Dictionary of the Bible*, ed. Katharine Doob Sakenfeld (Nashville: Abingdon Press, 2006–2009), 741.

[23] Matthew 21:33-45; 22:1-14; 23:1-25:46.

strong and constant, focused not upon the fate of humans after death, but on the fate of Israel and her promised land. The nation and land of the present world were far more important than what happened to an individual beyond the grave."[24]

The notion of afterlife punishment was not apparent in the biblical text. There is plenty of judgment for the wicked, but it is on earth. Sinners would be judged and the righteous would be justified in this life. Souls of the dead did not separate into heaven and hell. Both the righteous and the wicked went to Sheol, the underworld equivalent of Hades (Greek).[25] In the Bible, Sheol was sometimes a metaphor for the grave, sometimes it was an actual location beneath the earth where all the souls of the dead went, "a place of silence, darkness and oblivion."[26]

At best, there is a faint echo of hope through a few references in the Old Testament to some kind of "glory" in the afterlife,[27] but it is not defined with any clarity and is part of the package of afterlife doctrines that develop in the Intertestamental period and see reflected in the New Testament, and it is there we see a stronger definition of afterlife judgment and reward.

One of those doctrines developed between the testaments is that of resurrection. Maccabees plays an important part in that development because it marks one of the first strong faith affirmations of individuals being resurrected in their physical bodies after death to be with the Lord.

The Old Testament primarily treated resurrection as a metaphor for Israel's return from exile and diaspora and her reconstitution in the land that God had promised her. The most famous and obvious example of

---

[24] N. T. Wright, *The Resurrection of the Son of God: Christian Origins and the Question of God* (London: Society for Promoting Christian Knowledge, 2003), 99. He provides the following verses as evidence: Isa. 2:2–4; cf. Mic. 4:1–3, Isa. 11:1–9 ;42:1, 4; 61:1, 3; Ps. 72:1–4, 8, 12.

[25] For an in-depth examination of Sheol/Hades, see Brian Godawa, *When Giants Were Upon the Earth: The Watchers, the Nephilim, and the Biblical Cosmic War of the Seed*, (Los Angeles: Embedded Pictures Publishing, 2014), 99-101, 298-308.

[26] Kim Papaioannou, *The Geography of Hell in the Teaching of Jesus: Gehenna, Hades, the Abyss, the Outer Darkness Where There Is Weeping and Gnashing of Teeth* (Eugene, OR: Pickwick Publications, 2013), 87-88. Verses he uses to support this depressing vision of Sheol: Job 7:6-9; Eccl 9:5; Isa 26:14; Eccl 9:5; Ps. 6:5; Pss 115:17; 88:10–12; Isa 38:18; Job 17:13; Ps 88:5.

[27] See Psalm 49:15; 73:24: Job 19:25-27.

this is Ezekiel's vision of the Valley of Dry Bones where graves are opened and corpses are reconstituted with their flesh, sinew, and breath. Ezekiel explains this vision as a metaphor for Yahweh "bringing them back into the land of Israel" (Ezekiel 37:1-14).

Other passages some Christians think refer to a physical future resurrection of the living and the dead are also metaphors for Israel's reconstitution. Isaiah possesses the bulk of these passages, but Isaiah's context is as a prophetic warning of the impending Exile but simultaneously giving hope for Israel's ultimate return to the Land.[28] When the prophet says in Isaiah 26:19, "Your dead shall live; their bodies shall rise. You who dwell in the dust, awake and sing for joy!" he is speaking in context of a future return from the Assyrian Exile that was about to come upon Israel. Like Ezekiel's vision of resurrection, Isaiah here promises that Israel's "deadness" will not be forever. Yahweh will revive His chosen people.

Some orthodox Christian theologians exegete Daniel 12:2, one of the few possible explicit references to a future resurrection at the end of time, as being the fulfillment of Ezekiel's national restoration accomplished in Christ.[29] As Daniel had written, "Many of those who sleep in the dust of the earth shall awake, some to everlasting life, and some to shame and everlasting contempt." *Many* (Israelites) does not mean *all* (humanity). And *some* (Jews who received Messiah) would have everlasting life, while *some* (Jews who rejected Messiah) would have everlasting contempt.

Though Christians will point to some of these metaphorical resurrection passages as fulfilled in Christ's physical resurrection from the dead (Hosea 6:1-2; Isaiah 25:8; Psalm 16:8-11), that is a New Testament prophetic development not found in their original context. The New Testament-era Apostles have every authority to construct

---

[28] Isa 25:8; 26:13-19; 27:6; 52:1-2. See also Hosea 13:14.

[29] James B. Jordan, *The Handwriting on the Wall: A Commentary on the Book of Daniel* (Powder Springs, GA: American Vision, 2007), 615-624; Ken Gentry, "Resurrection in Daniel 12:1," PostmillennialWorldview.com posted November 21, 2014. https://postmillennialworldview.com/2014/11/21/resurrection-in-daniel-122/

those connections, but, as mentioned earlier, that constitutes an advancement or development of doctrine. And even then, these passages would not be references to a general resurrection of all humans who have ever lived at the end of time.

I am not saying the Jews had no concept of resurrection. They did. And they believed in the miraculous resurrections of individuals at the hands of Elijah and Elisha (1 Kings 17:17-24; 2 Kings 4:18-20). But these were *miraculous* exceptions. They did not consider the concept of a universal resurrection from the dead that would be a part of the New Covenant.[30] I am also not saying that the Bible does not teach an eschatological bodily resurrection, only that these passages do not teach it. The New Testament, as new revelation from God, does argue for an eschatological bodily resurrection of the living and the dead (John 5:25-29; 1 Corinthians 15:20-26).

The books of Maccabees mark one of the first examples of doctrinal development beyond the metaphor of national reconstitution and applied to individuals' physical resurrection. And this is important because it also marked a rejection of the Hellenistic doctrine that there was no resurrection of the dead. Although the Greeks maintained a belief in the soul's immortality, like the Hebrews, they too considered Hades (their word for the underworld) as the ultimate destination of the dead—also like the Hebrews, a place of meaningless existence.[31] But there was no return to the land of the living for the dead soul. As the Greek poet Aeschylus wrote, "When the dust has soaked up a man's blood, once he is dead there is no resurrection."[32]

In 2 Maccabees 6, we are presented with the heroic martyrdoms of a woman and her seven sons by Antiochus Epiphanes. They would not obey Antiochus and disavow their God's commands of Sabbath,

---

[30] John 5:28-29; Acts 24:15; 1 Corinthians 15:52; Revelation 20:12-13.

[31] Kim Papaioannou, *The Geography of Hell in the Teaching of Jesus: Gehenna, Hades, the Abyss, the Outer Darkness Where There Is Weeping and Gnashing of Teeth* (Eugene, OR: Pickwick Publications, 2013), 86.

[32] Cited in F. F. Bruce, *Paul Apostle of the Heart Set Free* (1977; reprint, Cumbria, UK: Paternoster, 2000), 247.

circumcision, and dietary laws. And they were put through gruesome and excruciating torture for their devotion. None of them recanted, but almost all of them appealed to the resurrection of their physical bodies as part of their hope for ultimate victory over their enemies.

The second martyred brother responded to his torturer before dying, "You dismiss us from this present life, but the King of the universe will raise us up to an everlasting renewal of life, because we have died for his laws" (2 Maccabees 7:9).

The third martyred brother, when threatened with dismemberment of his hands and tongue, said nobly, "I got these from Heaven, and…from him I hope to get them back again" (7:11).

The fourth martyred brother affirmed his hope of being raised, and proclaimed to his torturer, "But for you there will be no resurrection to life!" (7:14).

The fifth brother confirmed that their persecutor Antiochus would be punished in this life by God because "His mighty power will torture you and your descendants!" (7:17).

The mother of the brothers, also martyred, allegedly encouraged each of her seven male offspring with additional exhortations of their physical resurrections, that after their deaths, the Creator of the World "will in his mercy give life and breath back to you again" (7:23).

Of course, the books of the Maccabees are not Scripture, so their idea of bodily resurrection does not necessarily validate it any more than the notion of temple sacrifice for the dead in 2 Maccabees 12:39-45 supports the modern belief in Purgatory.[33] But it does illustrate an early understanding of bodily resurrection that Jesus and the Apostles would later affirm in the New Testament and signifies the origins of the two major schools of thought that would fight for control of the Jewish world of the New Testament: the Sadducees and the Pharisees.

---

33 For a refutation of the argument for Purgatory in 2 Maccabees, see Luke Wayne, "Purgatory and 2 Maccabees 12:39-45," Christian Apologetics and Research Ministry, CARM.org (January 31, 2017) https://carm.org/roman-catholicism/purgatory-and-2-maccabees-1239-45/

The Pharisees believed in both angels and a future Resurrection of the Dead but the Sadducees denied both altogether (Acts 23:6-8). Some argue that the Pharisee/Sadducee distinction may have originated in or around the time of the Maccabees, and that the doctrinal tone of 1 and 2 Maccabees embodies this distinction. First Maccabees contains no references to angels or resurrection, therefore reflecting what became the Sadducee tradition, while 2 Maccabees contains multiple references to both angels and resurrection, thus reflecting what became the Pharisee tradition. We will address all of these references throughout this book.[34]

One last interesting twist to this story of afterlife doctrines is 4 Maccabees, which devotes an obsessive fourteen chapters to the Eleazar's martyrdom and that of the mother and her seven sons. Most likely written in the first or second century BC, the book is more of a Hellenist philosophical treatise than a historical tale. It reflects a Jewish Hellenist worldview that elevates reason over emotion as humanity's supreme guide. It gives excruciating details of the torture instruments and their bodily effects on each of the seven sons and their mother at Antiochus Epiphanes's hands. In this Hellenist perspective, there is no longer reference to resurrection, but rather the Greek Platonic rejection of a body for the immortal soul. The reward of resurrection is replaced by the internal satisfaction of victorious endurance through suffering, with the rewards of heaven for the Jews and hellfire for Antiochus.

Ironically, the Hellenist view of 4 Maccabees subverted the anti-Hellenism of 1 and 2 Maccabees, as expressed in one of the many monologues attributed to the defiant Jewish martyrs.

> 4 Maccabees 9:7–9
> "Tyrant, put us to the test; and if you take our lives because of our religion, do not suppose that you can injure us by torturing us. For we, through this severe suffering and

[34] Angels: 2 Maccabees 2:21; 3:25-26; 3:33-34; 5:2-4; Resurrection: 2 Maccabees 7:1-42.

> endurance, shall have the prize of virtue and shall be with God, on whose account we suffer; but you, because of your bloodthirstiness toward us, will deservedly undergo from the divine justice eternal torment by fire."

The martyrdom of these faithful Jews would become a symbol of substitutionary atonement, the sacrifice of the innocent on behalf of the guilty nation. The one for the many. An obvious precursor to Jesus Christ.

> 4 Maccabees 17:21–22
> [The martyrs] having become, as it were, a ransom for the sin of our nation. And through the blood of those devout ones and their death as an atoning sacrifice, divine Providence preserved Israel that previously had been mistreated.

Chapter 2
The Nations

The Seleucids and Hellenism

The context of the Maccabees story is a Hellenistic world. The term *Hellenism* has its origin in the Greek empire of Alexander the Great. Alexander was an important part of God's prophetic plans he proclaimed through the prophet Daniel more than 250 years earlier. Let me explain that in more detail.

Alexander became king of Macedon in 336 BC at the young age of 20. Just before his father, Philip of Macedon, died, Philip had begun to unite Greece's independent city-states to attack their Leviathan enemy in the east, Persia. Alexander continued that foreign policy and proved to be an amazing military strategist. He swept east, conquering the Persian domain including Asia Minor, Egypt, the Levant, Mesopotamia, and all the way to India.

The ancient Jewish historian Josephus wrote about a fascinating encounter between Alexander and the Jewish high priest in Jerusalem on Alexander's way toward Persia. Jaddua, the high priest at the time, knew that the Greek kingdom would succeed the Medo-Persian kingdom because the prophet Daniel had predicted it, so he and a retinue of temple priests received Alexander with celebration, showing the conqueror that he was the fulfillment of their own Scriptures.

> Josephus, *Antiquities* 11.5 (337)
> And when the book of Daniel was showed him [Alexander], wherein Daniel declared that one of the Greeks should destroy the empire of the Persians, he

> supposed that himself was the person intended; and as he was then glad.[1]

Because of this encounter, the Jews enjoyed favor and tolerance of their laws by Alexander's own decree.

Daniel had described in several visions the order of kingdoms that would rule over Israel until Messiah would come. As interpreted by Daniel, King Nebuchadnezzar's dream (see Daniel 2) described them as metallic components of a large statue and, in Daniel's own dream (see Daniel 7) under King Belshazzar, as hybrid chaos monsters. The historical order was: Babylon, Media-Persia, Greece, and finally Rome.

Daniel described the Greek empire as a "kingdom of bronze that will rule over all the earth" (Daniel 2:39) and as "a leopard, with four wings of a bird on its back. And the beast had four heads, and dominion was given to it" (Daniel 7:6). Then in Daniel 8, the Greeks are symbolized as a male goat that attacks the Persians symbolized as a ram standing along a canal bank (Daniel 8:3-5). The goat "had a conspicuous horn between his eyes" (8:5), representing Alexander the Great, as the horns in Daniel symbolize powerful kings. The goat strikes the ram and breaks its two horns (the two kings of the Medo-Persian alliance), victoriously trampling the ram, just as Alexander broke the Persian kingdom and trampled it.

The historical accuracy of Daniel's prophecies are so precise that liberal theologians made up a conspiracy theory of Daniel's writing being *vaticinium ex eventu* ("prophecy from the event") in the days of the Maccabees rather than "before the event" in the days of Babylonian Exile. In other words, liberals presupposed without evidence that accurate prophecy is impossible. Therefore, Daniel's prophecies were so accurate in detail, they must have been written after the fact and made to look like they were written "before the fact." That would affirm their

[1] Flavius Josephus and William Whiston, *The Works of Josephus: Complete and Unabridged* (Peabody, MA: Hendrickson, 1987), 307.

anti-supernatural prejudice and discredit the Bible's historical reliability.[2]

In the chart below, the reader can see the repetition and overlap of prophetic symbols related to the Gentile kingdoms that rule Israel's history until the arrival of Messiah under ancient Rome. And that chronological timeline of Babylon, Persia, Greece, and Rome reflected history with profound precision.

Kings / Kingdoms	Daniel 2 Statue	Daniel 7 Hybrid Beasts	Daniel 8 Ram and Goat
Babylon	Head of gold 2:38	Lion with eagle's wings 7:4	
Medes and Persians	Chest and arms of silver 2:39	Bear with ribs in mouth 7:5	Ram along canal with two horns 8:3
Greeks	Middle and thighs of bronze 2:39	Leopard with 4 wings, 4 heads 7:6	Male goat from the west 8:5
Alexander the Great			A conspicuous horn, broken while strong 8:5-8
Alexander's 4 Successors			4 horns that replace broken horn 8:8
Antiochus IV Epiphanes			Little horn that attacks the "glorious land" (Israel) 8:9-14
Rome	Legs of iron, feet of iron and clay 2:40-41	Terrifying with iron teeth, 10 horns 7:7-8	The time of the end/end of days 12:4, 13

---

[2] For a scholarly introduction to the reliability of the book of Daniel and its prophecies, see Josh McDowell, *Daniel in the Critics Den* (San Bernardino, CA: Here's Life Publishers, Inc., 1979); Gleason L. Archer, *New International Encyclopedia of Bible Difficulties, Zondervan's Understand the Bible Reference Series* (Grand Rapids, MI: Zondervan Publishing House, 1982), 282–293; Norman L. Geisler, "Daniel, Dating Of," in *Baker Encyclopedia of Christian Apologetics, Baker Reference Library* (Grand Rapids, MI: Baker Books, 1999), 178–180.

Alexander is a key figure in Daniel's predictions, not just because he conquered the known civilized world but because he set the stage for Hellenization that would fashion the world in which Messiah could have worldwide impact unlike any other time in history. It's all about Jesus, folks.

Though Alexander was a conqueror, he sought to "civilize" his subjects by universally teaching them Greek culture and language. As noted earlier, the effect was the creation of a common language that overcame the division of segregated nations and peoples. This enabled more efficient and effective communication, social integration, education, and economic growth within the Hellenic kingdom.

Alexander founded the eponymous city of Alexandria, Egypt, which would house the world's largest multicultural library. At that location, Jewish scribes translated their Scriptures into Greek and introduced them to the entire world just eighty years later. The New Testament was also written in Greek, enabling Christians to share the Gospel of Jesus Christ more rapidly and effectively than any other language could have—to both rich and poor, high and low, from all walks of life—all over the world. The fact that everyone in the world of their day spoke Greek is what enabled God's Word, written in Greek, to spread so wide and with such alacrity. This is not to justify any criminal or oppressive actions of the Hellenistic empire, but certainly to appreciate the power of Providence. What oppressors meant for evil, God used for good.

The Hellenizing goal of cultural dominance would ultimately bring the inclusive empire into conflict with Israel's exclusive culture. Greece, of course, worshipped an inclusive pantheon of gods, while Israel exclusively worshipped the singular Creator God, Yahweh. And Israel's peculiar practice of identity separation from the Gentile nations, even while living within them, would also become a thorn in the flesh of any imperial attempt, from Babylon to Rome, to enforce cultural and religious uniformity.

But next in the timeline is Alexander's untimely death to disease at the young age of 30 while in Babylon. Daniel's vision described this interruptive event as the conspicuous horn on the goat being "broken when he was strong" (Daniel 8:8). In other words, Alexander died at the height of his power.

Then Daniel 8:8 says that out of that goat's head "there came up four conspicuous horns toward the four winds of heaven." This reveals the political consequences of Alexander's death. Alexander's six generals, called the Diadochi, then quarreled over his vast kingdom, which stretched across the "four winds of heaven"—north, south, east and west. After 20 years, the internecine warfare ended with one of those six generals ruling each of the four major kingdoms ("four horns"). Cassander held Macedonia and Greece; Lysimachus had Thrace and Bithnyia; Ptolemy ruled Egypt, the Levant/Judea, and Petra; and Seleucus governed Syria, Babylonia, and the vast eastern region to India.

The Greek Ptolemies in the south formed an Egyptian dynasty ruling from Alexandria, while the Greek Seleucids to Judea's north, headquartered in Antioch, became a Syrian dynasty. These two kingdoms would then dominate the prophetic focus of Daniel 11. Daniel refers to these dynastic kings as the kings of the north and south (see the chart of Daniel 11 prophecies and their historical fulfillments in Chapter 1 under "Maccabees and Daniel").

Israel would trade hands between the two rival kingdoms battling for control of the Levant as the intersection of access between the four points of the compass. The northern Seleucids in Syria and southern Egyptian Ptolemies would engage in six different wars—called the Syrian Wars—with each other over the next 100 years until Rome put a stop to it in 168 BC, the time of my Maccabees novels.

The Roman Republic had been on the ascendant for many years and had recently won its own war with the Seleucids a decade earlier, forcing Antiochus III, king of Seleucia, to sign a treaty of submission. So, when Antiochus IV sought to invade Egypt—Rome's major source of grain—a second time in 168 BC, Rome sent a political envoy, Caius Popilius Laenas, to issue Antiochus an ultimatum. In one of the most well-known moments of Roman history, called the Day of Eleusis, Popilius met Antiochus outside Alexandria in the city of Eleusis. Hellenist historian Polybius tells the story of Antiochus's humiliation:

> Polybius, *Histories, Fragments of Book XXIX*
> When Antiochus [IV Epiphanes] had advanced to attack Ptolemy [VI Philometer] in order to possess himself of Pelusium, he was met by the Roman commander Gaius Popilius Laenas. Upon the king greeting him from some distance, and holding out his right hand to him, Popilius answered by holding out the tablets which contained the decree of the Senate, and bade Antiochus read that first: not thinking it right, I suppose, to give the usual sign of friendship until he knew the mind of the recipient, whether he were to be regarded as a friend or foe. On the king, after reading the dispatch, saying that he desired to consult with his friends on the situation, Popilius did a thing which was looked upon as exceedingly overbearing and insolent. Having a vine stick in his hand, he drew a circle round Antiochus with it, and ordered him to give his answer to the letter before he stepped out of that circumference. The king was taken aback by this haughty proceeding. After a brief interval of embarrassed silence, he replied he would do whatever the Romans demanded. Then Popilius and his colleagues shook him by the hand, and one and all greeted him with warmth.[3]

This historical event was foretold in Daniel 11 as the incitement of anger that resulted in Antiochus IV taking destructive action against Israel, the people of the holy covenant:

---

[3] Polybius, *Histories* (Medford, MA: Macmillan, 1889), 405–406.

> Daniel 11:29–30
> "At the time appointed he [Antiochus] shall return and come into the south [Egypt], but it shall not be this time as it was before [Antiochus' first attack on Egypt]. For ships of Kittim [Rome] shall come against him, and he shall be afraid and withdraw, and shall turn back and be enraged and take action against the holy covenant [nation of Israel].

Daniel then describes Antiochus's persecution of the Jews, which includes setting up a graven image in the Jerusalem temple (11:31-35), which we will address later.

But Daniel does not end his prophecy there. He then describes a different king, who comes later to "do as he wills" (Daniel 11:36). This reference to a willful king is a phrase Daniel used of other tyrant kings: Alexander the Great (11:3), Cyrus the Great (8:4), and Antiochus III the Great (11:16). This new willful king of 11:36 is not Antiochus Epiphanes, but a future one taht leads into Daniel 12 and the "time of the end," which we will also address later.

So the last Seleucid king to which Daniel refers in chapter 11 is Antiochus IV Epiphanes, who is a prominent figure in the story of the Maccabees. We will take a closer look at Antiochus in Chapter 3: The Characters.

Scythians and Amazons

The reader of all my Chronicles series will notice that female warriors are rare to the stories, the exceptions being in the older stories of the primeval history of Genesis 1-11, Noah, Enoch, and Gilgamesh. The reason is that the primeval history that precedes Abraham is more mythopoeic in its narrative genre. That is to say, it is not strictly history and not strictly myth. It uses elements of both genres.

It is more what Evangelical scholar William Lane Craig calls, "mytho-history." Myth here is not defined as false or made-up stories, but stories told by a culture—fictional or non-fictional—that express that culture's values and worldview.

Craig explains,

> We retain the term "history" in the title of this first unit of the Bible—the Primeval History—because, on the one hand, it arranges themes along a time continuum using cause and effect and generally uses historical narrative as the literary medium for communication. On the other hand, those themes themselves are the same ones explored elsewhere in the ancient Near East in mythological literature…[4]

Craig appeals to the Trojan War, as described in Homer's *Iliad*, as an example of mytho-history. Homer described an historical event but told the story through the worldview of the Greek gods and fates.

Considering the more mythopoeic nature of Genesis's primeval history, I felt free to use more creative license in having some female warriors in my earlier novels of Enoch and Noah (mytho-history).[5] But as the storyline of my Chronicles series progresses, it becomes more historical and less mythopoeic, therefore focusing on the reality of male warriors in a patriarchal culture. The more physical the combat, the less likely women could withstand the scientific realities of a male's larger size, heavier bone structure, stronger musculature, and endurance. Sure, there could have been exceptions, but as a rule, women were not warriors in the ages of Stone, Bronze, and Iron.

There is, however, an historical exception I discovered wherein I could somewhat equalize that general male superiority through technology, much like guns can be equalizers in the modern world.

Enter, the Amazons.

---

[4] William Lane Craig, *In Quest of the Historical Adam: A Biblical and Scientific Exploration* (Grand Rapids, MI: Eerdmans, 2021), Epub Edition.

[5] *Enoch Primordial* and *Noah Primeval* of Chronicles of the Nephilim series.

The image of female Amazon warriors, at the same time both physically beautiful and deadly in battle, had captivated much of Greco-Roman imagination, libido, and mythology. As scholar Adrienne Mayor writes,

> Every great champion of myth—Heracles, Theseus, Achilles—proved his valor by overcoming powerful warrior queens and their armies of women. Those glorious struggles against foreign man-killers were recounted in oral tales and written epics and illustrated in countless artworks throughout the Greco-Roman world. Famous historical figures, among them King Cyrus of Persia, Alexander the Great, and the Roman general Pompey, also tangled with Amazons.[6]

Mayor has argued that whatever historical reality lies behind the Amazons, they were probably mythologized to express the diametrically opposite picture of the role of ancient Greek women in society to show the Greek social order's superiority. Greek women were mostly house-bound, domestic, submissive, and expected to be sexually loyal to their husbands within an extremely patriarchal system. In contrast, Amazons were idealized as outdoors-oriented, hunters, wild, sexually promiscuous, against marriage, and socially matriarchal. This was why the Greek heroes always conquered Amazons in their mythic battles. Such warrior women were an unavoidable narrative fantasy of violating social taboos used to illustrate the unnatural uncivilized societies outside of Greece.[7]

Mayor links the Amazon myth to the historical Scythian tribes in the Northeastern Steppes surrounding the Black Sea in what is now modern-day Ukraine and Russia. It turns out that the Amazon legends

---

[6] Adrienne Mayor, *The Amazons: Lives and Legends of Warrior Women Across the Ancient World* (Princeton, NJ: Princeton University Press, 2014), 11.

[7] See also Cynthia Eller, *The Myth of Matriarchal Prehistory: Why an Invented Past Won't Give Women a Future* (Boston: Beacon Press, 2001), 178.

focused heavily on the Black Sea area, and the actual Scythian tribes provided the evidence for the existence of female warriors.

The Scythians were a nomadic people who migrated to the Black Sea region during the 9th and 8th centuries BC. Beginning around 653 BC and for a brief 28 years, they dominated a region that extended far east and south all the way to the edge of Mesopotamia and the Caspian Sea.

The Greeks and surrounding empires considered the Scythians to be barbarians because of their reputation for wildness in living and in battle. They smoked pot (hemp), tattooed their skin, and were more sexually promiscuous and less monogamous than the Greeks.[8] Some classical writers expanded this reputation by mythologizing tribes of Amazons, called "man-killers" (*Oiorpata*), who either interacted with the Scythians or were exceptional members of Scythian tribes. As the stories went, Amazons were exclusively female tribes who separated themselves, having sex with neighboring males, only to create offspring, either keeping the baby girls to rear or crippling the baby boys so that they could not take control of the female tribe.[9]

Scythians were an equestrian culture that historian Edwin Yamauchi explains were among history's earliest mounted archers. They became known for their special skills of firing their bows backwards while in full gallop away from an enemy. Though they used other weapons such as battleaxes and swords, the bow-and-arrow was their dominant form of combat and gave them a distinct advantage.[10]

This was also why women were allegedly able to fight in battle. The technology of both horse and bow equalized the soldier's power and displaced the act of battle away from the body. Most women would not have a chance facing a man's superior physical strength in battle with swords and battleaxes, but a woman on horseback was enhanced

---

8 Adrienne Mayor, *The Amazons,* 95-154.

9 Adrienne Mayor, *The Amazons,* 155-159. Renate Rolle, trans., F.G. Walls, *The World of the Scythians* (Berkeley, CA: University of California Press, 1989), 86.

10 Edwin Yamauchi, *Foes From the Northern Frontier: Invading Hordes from the Russian Steppes* (Eugene, OR: Wipf and Stock, 1982), 91.

in both power and speed to a man's near-equivalent. And aiming a deadly projectile required only enough muscle strength to draw a bowstring, making a woman almost as deadly as any male in like circumstance.

In a nomadic culture, there is a greater need for men and women to share social, economic, and military responsibilities. Recent archaeological revelations of hundreds of Scythian graves across the Eurasian steppes have revealed about twenty percent were armed females with horse trappings, the equivalent of male warrior burials. Mayor concludes that hunter-warrior horsewomen were a historical reality "from the Western Black Sea to northern China."[11]

This more egalitarian society is also reflected in the fact that the Scythians practically invented the trousers. Spending long hours on horseback led to the invention of leather pants for skin protection of both men and women, making their dress less gender-distinct than Greek culture's and therefore another offense to the Greek natural order.[12]

The Scythians show up in the background of biblical history. Yamauchi explains that the Hebrew term *Ashkenaz* in the Old Testament is a designation of Scythia.[13] He concludes the Scythians were mercenaries who were part of the invading "enemy from the north" prophesied by Jeremiah about King Nebuchadnezzar raiding Jerusalem in 633 BC (Jeremiah 1:14-15)[14] and destroying Assyria (Zephaniah 2:13).[15]

And during the days of the prophet Daniel, the Persians subjugated the Scythians and ended up fighting *with* them against the Greeks in 499

---

[11] Renate Rolle, trans., F. G. Walls, *The World of the Scythians* (Berkeley, CA: University of California Press, 1989), 89. Feminist Adrienne Mayor selectively chooses data to conclude as high as 37% armed female burials. Adrienne Mayor, *The Amazons,* 63-64.

[12] Adrienne Mayor, *The Amazons,* 191-197.

[13] Genesis 10:3; 1 Chronicles 1:6; Jeremiah 51:27.

[14] See also Jeremiah 4:6; 6:1, 22.

[15] Edwin Yamauchi, *Foes*, 63, 87-91, 99.

BC.[16] The name of Bethshean, a city in Galilee of Israel, was changed to Scythopolis because of a Scythian invasion and settlement in Israel.[17] That very city would later be favorable toward the Maccabees during their war with the Seleucids.

Though the Scythian tribes and their influence had been significantly reduced by the time of the Maccabees, they were not without presence. I depict the Scythians, Arabs, and even Amazons as part of the mercenary forces used by Antiochus, because as G. T. Griffith shows, Seleucid mercenaries included Scythians, Arabs, Jews, Mysians, Gauls, Thracians, and other nationalities from Asia Minor.[18]

The books of Maccabees describe General Apollonius as gathering a "large force from Samaria" to fight against Israel with his Seleucid army (1 Maccabees 3:10). The Seleucid general Lysias is described as enlisting mercenaries at the battle of Beth-Zur (1 Maccabees 4:35) and other mercenary forces came to him later "from other kingdoms and from islands of the seas" (1 Maccabees 6:29). It is not unreasonable to assume that the Scythians/Amazons may have been a part of King Antiochus's horse-mounted cavalry.

During the time of the Maccabees, the Scythians were considered the cruelest of barbarians. During the high priesthood of Menelaus, some Jewish council officials were executed for causing an uprising in Tyre. The Egyptian ruler "sentenced to death those unfortunate men, who would have been freed uncondemned, if they had pleaded *even before Scythians*" (2 Maccabees 4:47). In other words, the king was so barbaric, that his actions were compared to the Scythians' cruelty.

Third Maccabees 7:5 tells of some Jews treating apostates with "a cruelty more savage than the law of the Scythians." And finally, 4 Maccabees 10:7 describes the Scythian-like torture of one of the seven Jewish sons martyred by Antiochus Epiphanes's forces: "They broke

---

16 Edwin Yamauchi, *Foes*, 100.

17 Edwin Yamauchi, *Foes*, 84.

18 G. T. Griffith, *The Mercenaries of the Hellenistic World* (Cambridge: Cambridge University Press, 1935),

his fingers, arms, legs and elbows. …they tore off his skin and scalped him with their fingertips in the Scythian fashion."

Yamauchi summarizes the Scythians' bizarre and savage practices as described by the Greek historian Herodotus:

> 1. The Scythians drank the blood of the first enemy killed.
> 2. They carried the heads of their victims to their chiefs. They scalped their enemies and used these scalps as "napkins".
> 3. They used the skins of their victims to cover their quivers.
> 4. They drank from the skulls of their victims.
> 5. They practiced blood brotherhood by drinking each other's blood mixed with wine.
> 6. The Scythians "bathed" in the vapor from heated hemp seeds.
> 7. When their king died, they sacrificed one of his concubines and several servants.
> 8. After a year they commemorated his death by sacrificing fifty servants and fifty horses.[19]

By the time of the New Testament, the Scythian population was all but replaced by the nomadic Sarmatians, but their reputation had lived on as being the most barbaric of savages. The one place Paul's letters mention the Scythians is in Colossians 3:11: "Here there is not Greek and Jew, circumcised and uncircumcised, barbarian, <u>Scythian</u>, slave, free; but Christ is all, and in all." In this context of contrasting opposites, Paul is virtually referring to Scythians as more barbaric than barbarians.

---

[19] Edwin Yamauchi, *Foes*, 111, from Herodotus, *Histories* 4.64-75.

Chapter 3
The Characters

Judah Maccabee

The title character of the *Judah Maccabee* novels retains the Jewish pronunciation. In the Greek manuscripts of the books we have, his Greek name is Judas Maccabeus. This either reflects a Greek translation of the original or, more likely, Hellenism's effect on Jewish names. For example, when Alexander first met with the Jewish leaders in Jerusalem, around 329 BC, in exchange for a degree of autonomy, they had agreed to name all their children born the next year "Alexander." To this day, the name Alexander is popular in Jewish communities, and back then it opened the door for cultural infiltration.[1]

This is why, in the novel, I begin with the Greek name of Judas to show his embrace of Hellenism. But when he and his family reject the Seleucid powers, Judas changes his name back to the Jewish original, Judah, to express his return to orthodox Judaism from Hellenism.

The title "Maccabee," though it designated Judas's family as well as their movement of resistance against the empire, was originally a nickname for Judas alone. Scholars are not entirely sure what it means, but the consensus is "hammerer" or "hammer," as in the crushing defeat that he gave the Seleucids in their war.[2] But Bible scholar Bruce Gore has claimed that the word *maccabee* was also "an acrostic of Hebrew

---

1 "Alexander the Great," JewishHistory.org https://www.jewishhistory.org/alexander-the-great/

2 Robert C. Kashow, "Judas Maccabeus," in *The Lexham Bible Dictionary*, ed. John D. Barry et al. (Bellingham, WA: Lexham Press, 2016).

letters standing for the Deuteronomic phrase: 'Who is like you among the gods, O LORD' (mi kamocha ba'elim hashem)."[3]

The books of the Maccabees tell us almost nothing of Judas's life before the Maccabean uprising. He is simply introduced in 1 Maccabees 2:4 as one of Mattathias's five sons, and that he was "a mighty warrior from his youth" (1 Maccabees 2:66). On his deathbed, Mattathias appoints Judas to command their guerilla army against the Seleucids, which indicates a leadership skill in Judas that is superior to that of his elder brothers Simon and John. Though middle child, Judas was certainly a mighty warrior and a smart tactician of war.

His father Mattathias is described as a "priest of the family of Joarib" (1 Maccabees 2:1), and while it is not uncommon for sons to follow in their fathers' footsteps, it is not universal. So I chose to make Judas the spotted sheep of his family, and I begin his story as a Hellenist who has joined King Antiochus's Jewish mercenary forces, thus alienating from his Jewish tradition and devout family. This is a way to show the transformation of a Hellenist back to a Hasidim (or Hasidean) Jew separated from the Gentile nations as holy. By the time Judas rises up, he is aligned with his father and brothers, as depicted in the books of the Maccabees.

There are virtually no references to the wives of the brothers Maccabee in the texts, a common feature of male-centric storytelling. But there is no reason to believe they were all bachelors. One verse in 2 Maccabees 14:25 depicts Nicanor, a friendly Seleucid general, urging Judas to marry and have children. But this event occurs long after the events of the temple cleansing. The text says, "So Judas married, settled down and shared the common life." Shortly after that, the war between the Maccabees and Seleucids returned. Of course, such a marriage would not discount the possibility of Judas being married before the war

---

[3] Bruce W. Gore, *Historical and Chronological Context of the Bible* (Trafford Publishing, 2006), 10.24. From Exodus 15:11.

to a woman who might end up as one of the multitude of civilian casualties that occurred under Antiochus's reign of terror.

In the novels, Judas's participation in the Greek king's mercenary forces was not an entirely fictional fabrication. Part of the Hellenization process included the assumption of Jewish mercenaries into the king's army. In fact, the insurrection incident in the novel where Judas helps to suppress his own rioting countrymen was based on an incident that admittedly happened later in the Maccabean period.

First Maccabees 10:36-37 tells of Jonathan Maccabee sending 30,000 Jewish warriors to Antioch to join the king's guard. Shortly after, 3,000 Jewish "mighty men" arrive at Antioch to celebrate the Greek king and an uprising occurs.

> 1 Maccabees 11:45-48
> And those from the city gathered together in the middle of the city to the number of one hundred and twenty thousand men, and they wanted to kill the king. And the king fled into the palace; and those from the city took control of the streets of the city, and they began to make war. And the king called for the Judeans for help, and they gathered to him all together and spread out in the city and killed in the city in that day up to one hundred thousand. And they burned the city and took many spoils on that day and delivered the king.[4]

Though the novel sometimes displaces events in time, my goal was to avoid complete fabrication by rooting events in some historical reference as much as possible.

One instance in which I used creative license was the famous whip sword, Rahab, that reoccurs throughout the Chronicles series of novels. Fashioned from "heavenly metal" in Eden, this unique fictional weapon works like a whip, but its ten-foot lash is made of highly flexible metal

---

[4] Rick Brannan et al., eds., *The Lexham English Septuagint* (Bellingham, WA: Lexham Press, 2012), 1 Mac 11:44–52.

that can cut through most anything. Various characters have had the privilege of using it through my Chronicles Series, including Lamech, Caleb, and Ittai the Gittite, the latter of whom placed it in the Jerusalem temple for safe-keeping at the end of the novel *David Ascendant*.

When the temple is rebuilt after its destruction by Babylon, the sword is returned to its secret location and the abominable Apollonius, who later desolates the temple, ultimately discovers it. Judas, in the *Judah Maccabee* novels, then seizes the sword from Apollonius in the battle of Lebonah Pass. I worked this into the historical reference in 1 Maccabees 3:12 of Apollonius having an infamous yet undescribed sword taken by Judas: "Judas took the sword of Apollonius, and used it in battle the rest of his life." I tied this together with another event that happened in a dream Judas had in 2 Maccabees. In the dream, a Jew named Jeremiah gave Judas a special sword, "a golden sword, and as he gave it he addressed him thus: 'Take this holy sword, a gift from God, with which you will strike down your adversaries'" (2 Maccabees 15:15-16).

The Brothers Maccabee

There is not much description of Judas's four brothers in the Maccabees books. But one passage gives their nicknames:

> 1 Maccabees 2:2–5 (LES)
> And to him there were five sons: John, who was called Gaddi; Simon, who was called Thassi; Judas, who was called Maccabeus; Eleazar, who was called Avaran; and Jonathan, who was called Apphus.

Unfortunately, these nicknames are not understood with certainty, but scholars have made educated guesses based on etymology and context. I chose the following interpretations of their nicknames to create their characters:[5]

John – Gaddi, "the Fortunate." As the eldest, it would make sense he was a fortunate one, but ironically, his father Mattathias did not chose him to lead the forces, which hints at a less-than-stellar intelligence or leadership compared with his juniors. So, how could he be fortunate? I made his fortune be his size and strength. Others would look upon this specimen of physical prowess and consider him fortunate.

Simon – Thassi, "The Wise." Simon was the second eldest. On his deathbed, Mattathias ordered Simon to be a "father" to Judas in the war through his "wise counsel" (1 Maccabees 2:65). He would become leader of the forces later in the battles of the Maccabees against the Seleucids. So, I made him a brilliant battle strategist for the brothers. More brain than brawn.

Eleazar – Avaran, "The Piercer." Eleazar, the second youngest, was given this nickname, no doubt later in the war because he died in the heroic act of killing a war elephant in the battle of Beth-Zechariah sometime after cleansing the temple (1 Maccabees 6:43-47). He did so by piercing the elephant in the belly with a spear, whereupon the giant beast fell upon Eleazar, crushing him. Unfortunately, it was an error on Eleazar's part because he had mistakenly thought it was the king's elephant.

The writer of 1 Maccabees sought to redeem Eleazar's apparent failure by describing that act as part of an attack so "fierce" that the Greek forces fled in retreat, thus giving Eleazar "an everlasting name" (6:44). I used this incident in an earlier battle of the novel to condense the timeline for plot purposes and used his daring feat as an expression of his expert skill with the javelin. Because Judas also gave Eleazar the

---

[5] I used Wikipedia for these names because it was the best gathering of all the various interpretations available of the nicknames. I usually avoid Wikipedia for research because of its politicization of many issues, making it an unreliable source. But not all information is political and, in this case, it was a good collection.

privilege of reading Torah to the troops before another battle (2 Maccabees 8:23), I made Eleazar spiritually zealous in his youth.

Jonathan – Apphus, "The Dissembler." Because dissembling carries the negative denotation of putting on a false appearance or façade, I decided to make him the politician of the five brothers. This would make sense of the fact that, though Jonathan was the youngest, his brothers voted him to take over leadership of the Jewish forces when Judas was killed (1 Maccabees 9:28-31)! Ultimately, Jonathan became the nation's high priest (1 Maccabees 10:18-20). Only someone skilled at persuading the masses could provide that kind of political leadership and influence.

But some scholars believe the newly formed Essenes referred to Jonathan as "the Wicked Priest" who would split from the Maccabean Hasmoneans and settle the community of Qumran to leave us the Dead Sea Scrolls.[6] The Wicked Priest was an insulting nickname given to the high priest in Jerusalem who was considered illegitimate compared with the Essenes' own candidate, their "Teacher of Righteousness."

Eleazar the Scribe

Eleazar the scribe is a real historical character in the books of the Maccabees and a mentor figure for Judas in the novels. Though I have no historical proof of such a connection, it was certainly possible that they may have known each other since both were from priestly families in Jerusalem.

In the books of 1-4 Maccabees, Eleazar plays a significant role as a martyr who inspires other Jews to stand firm against Antiochus's persecution. He was a 90-year-old scribe and priest,[7] well-trained in Torah and, because of his age and reputation, was "familiar to many of those around the tyrant," Antiochus (4 Maccabees 5:4).

---

[6] David Noel Freedman and Jeffrey C. Geoghegan, "Another Stab at the Wicked Priest," James H. Charlesworth, Ed., *The Bible and the Dead Sea Scrolls Volume Two: The Dead Sea Scrolls and the Qumran Community* (Waco, TX: Baylor University Press, 2006), 17.

[7] 2 Maccabees 6:24.

As a scribe, Eleazar would have prestigious wisdom, influence, and status in Judea. The *Anchor Yale Bible Dictionary* explains scribal identity this way:

> The scribe is not simply a scholar or teacher in the modern mold, but a high official, advisor to the governing class, and international ambassador and traveler. The foundation for the scribes' social leadership is not birth or wealth but knowledge of discipline (education, culture), judgment, and proverbs (parables, similitudes).[8]

Second Maccabees 6, 3 Maccabees 6, and 4 Maccabees 5-6 describe Eleazar's eventual martyrdom.

King Antiochus had decreed that his whole kingdom should be unified as one people and that the Jews should abandon their customs of circumcision, dietary laws, Sabbath, and sacrifice. In Judea, Antiochus ordered Eleazar and others to eat pork and food sacrificed to idols. Though 1 Maccabees claims that Antiochus IV was not in Jerusalem for Eleazar's martyrdom, 2-4 Maccabees indicate he was there as detailed in verbal interactions between Antiochus and Eleazar during the gruesome tortures. Seleucid officials beat him, flogged him and put him on the rack, but the old scribe would not eat pork. They tried to force him to eat it, but he spit it out. Other Jews pleaded with him to pretend to eat pork, while actually eating kosher meat, that he might live. But he stood in his moral integrity and refused until he was executed.

Though 3 and 4 Maccabees are not considered historical, they served as ancient creative license for me as I drew from all these texts for the novel.

---

[8] Anthony J. Saldarini, "Scribes," in *The Anchor Yale Bible Dictionary*, ed. David Noel Freedman (New York: Doubleday, 1992), 1014.

Solomonia and the Seven Sons of Sacrifice

The other martyrs featured in the novels appear at a crucial turning point in the story because they are featured as such in the books of the Maccabees. One particular woman and her seven sons' family being tortured is described in shocking and grisly detail.[9] I drew from these narratives for the equally disturbing scenes in the novels in order to maintain historical verisimilitude.

Women who circumcised their sons were forced to hang their infants from their necks and were cast off the city walls to their deaths.[10] According to the texts above, these faithful Jews were stripped, beaten, scalped, thumb-screwed, put on the rack and the wheel, forced into cauldrons and frying pans, attached with claws to a catapult, had their limbs dislocated, dismembered, or torn from their sockets, disemboweled, decapitated, tongues cut out, drained of blood, and put to the fire. Yet none of them would disobey Yahweh by eating the forbidden meat commanded by King Antiochus.

Fourth Maccabees 12 tells the incident of the last of the seven brothers asking to be released to speak to the king as if he was recanting. But he only used the opportunity to curse the "ungodly tyrant" and assured him he would be punished "in the present life and in death" with "eternal fire and tortures" for his beastly profane behavior (4 Maccabees 12:12, 19).

Though these tortures are gruesome to read, they serve as a necessary picture of the serious cost of obedience to God and would ultimately become an inspiration for the Christians martyred in the first and subsequent centuries.

Though none of the Maccabees books name the mother and her seven sons, there is an Eastern tradition that links them as students of Eleazar the scribe, who was also martyred, and names the mother

---

9 1 Maccabees 1:54-64; 2 Maccabees 7:1-42; and 4 Maccabees 8-12.

10 1 Maccabees 1:60-61; 2 Maccabees 6:10; 4 Maccabees 4:25.

Solomonia and her sons Habim, Antonin, Guriah, Eleazar, Eusebon, Hadim, and Marcellus.[11]

Antiochus IV Epiphanes

The coming king foretold in Daniel's prophecy (Daniel 11:21-35) as a "contemptible" (ESV), "despicable" (NASB95), or "vile" person (NKJV) who would eventually bring about the "abomination of desolation" (v. 31) is also symbolized as "a little horn" that would grow out of Alexander's broken reign (Daniel 8:8-9) and grow powerful enough to defy Yahweh and oppress his holy people (8:9-14).[12]

That is why this story of the Maccabees is so important to the unfolding of God's plan to bring forth the Seed of the Woman that would crush the Serpent's head—the very storyline of all three of my Chronicles series of novels (Genesis 3:15). That despicable and vile little horn was none other than Antiochus IV Epiphanes, the Seleucid king in Syria.

As 1 Maccabees relates, Antiochus IV Epiphanes began his reign in the 137th "year of the Greeks," about 175 BC. He was the youngest son of Antiochus III the Great, so he was not heir to the throne. He usurped the crown through political manipulation, just as Daniel had prophesied:

> Daniel 11:21 (NASB95)
> A despicable person will arise, on whom the honor of kingship has not been conferred, but he will come in a time of tranquility and seize the kingdom by intrigue.

To understand the "intrigue" that Antiochus IV used to "seize" or usurp the crown, we must understand the historical situation. The Republic of Rome would require the son of a king who was under their

---

[11] http://www.holytrinityorthodox.com/calendar/los/August/01-03.htm

[12] Horns are a common prophetic symbol of kingship or rulers. There is another "little horn" that shows up in Daniel 7:20-21, 24-25. This is a different king than Antiochus Epiphanes, and he appears in the last kingdom of Rome. The Beast of Revelation matches that little horn of Daniel: Revelation 13:5-7; 17:9-10. For a full narrative depiction of this fulfillment, see my series, Chronicles of the Apocalypse.

control to be held hostage in Rome to ensure the client king's compliance. As an Italian mobster might put it, "You get outta line, we gotta your son." Antiochus IV had the unfortunate circumstance to be one of those hostages when his father was king. But later, Antiochus used that hostage experience to his benefit. Commentator Robert Doran explains Antiochus IV's intriguing kingdom situation:

> After the Romans decisively defeated Antiochus III at the battle of Magnesia (190 BCE), this youngest son [Antiochus IV] was handed over to the Romans as a hostage. Antiochus III was succeeded in 187 BCE by his older son, Seleucus IV. Around 176, the Romans exchanged Antiochus [IV] for Seleucus IV's son Demetrius [because he was son of the new king]. On Seleucus IV's death in 175 BCE, Antiochus [IV] seized the opportunity to gain control of the kingdom in place of his brother's son.[13]

But Antiochus's previous stay in Rome was also fortuitous in he received an education in the Roman way of politics and war. He would know his ultimate opponent well.

> Daniel 11:23
> And from the time that an alliance is made with him he shall act deceitfully, and he shall become strong with a small people.

As this prophecy predicts, Antiochus was in alliance with Rome because of Rome's support for him when he came to power. But in 170 BC, Egypt demanded Coele-Syria back from Antiochus in a territorial dispute. Antiochus's capital city, Antioch, was in Coele-Syria and he would not wait for such a personal attack to occur. So he consolidated

---

[13] Robert Doran, "The First Book of Maccabees," in *New Interpreter's Bible*, ed. Leander E. Keck, vol. 4 (Nashville: Abingdon Press, 1994–2004), 31.

his forces in 169 BC and invaded Egypt first in what would be called the Sixth Syrian War with King Ptolemy VI of Egypt.[14]

But Ptolemy could not stand against Antiochus. His own advisors betrayed him and Antiochus swept in and took Ptolemy VI prisoner. But after he did so, the city of Alexandria installed Ptolemy's younger brother, Ptolemy VIII Euergetes II, on the throne. Angered by this affront, Antiochus plotted with his prisoner Ptolemy VI against the installed opponent, and left to support Ptolemy VI as king in Memphis in a counter to Euergetes's claim. But eventually, the Ptolemy brother kings became allies and united over Egypt, which spoiled Antiochus's hopes of control.

Daniel foretold all of this [my explanations in brackets].

> Daniel 11:25–28
> And he [Antiochus IV of Syria] shall stir up his power and his heart against the king of the south [Ptolemy VI of Egypt] with a great army. And the king of the south [Ptolemy] shall wage war with an exceedingly great and mighty army, but he shall not stand, for plots shall be devised against him. Even those who eat his food shall break him. His [Ptolemy's] army shall be swept away, and many shall fall down slain.
>
> And as for the two kings [Antiochus and Ptolemy VI], their hearts shall be bent on doing evil [plotting against Ptolemy Euregetes]. They shall speak lies at the same table, but to no avail [the Egyptian Ptolemy brothers unite], for the end is yet to be at the time appointed.

On his way back home to Syria, Antiochus stopped off in Jerusalem and plundered the temple's treasury, which the prophet Daniel describes as imposing or "working his will":

---

[14] The rest of this section on Daniel's prophecies fulfilled in Antiochus Epiphanes is drawn from Bruce W. Gore, *Historical and Chronological Context of the Bible* (Trafford Publishing, 2006), 10.19-23.

> Daniel 11:28
> And he [Antiochus IV] shall return to his land with great wealth, but his heart shall be set against the holy covenant [Israel]. And he shall work his will and return to his own land [Syria].

Antiochus IV's first invasion of Egypt was very costly for the Seleucid king, who often pillaged temples as repositories of wealth to pay for his enterprises. Antiochus took the golden altar from the holy temple, as well as the famous Menorah lampstand and table of the Presence, besides all the gold and silver temple utensils and any other hidden treasures he could find (1 Maccabees 1:20-23).

The prophet Daniel explains what would happen next. A year later, in 168 BC, Antiochus returned to Egypt to finish what he started and take the city of Alexandria. However, Rome would not tolerate this and sent an emissary, Caius Popilius Laenas, to put a stop to the Seleucid advance. This was the infamous incident where Popilius drew the line in the sand and told Antiochus to give him an answer of submission to Rome before he crossed it. If Syria did not pull back from Egypt, they would be at war with Rome. Not a cheerful prospect for Antiochus. Here is how Daniel described it:

> Daniel 11:29
> At the time appointed he [Antiochus IV] shall return and come into the south [Egypt again], but it shall not be this time as it was before. For ships of Kittim [Rome] shall come against him, and he [Antiochus] shall be afraid and withdraw…

So, Antiochus obeyed Rome and returned to Syria. But upon hearing of a possible Jewish uprising in Jerusalem, Antiochus became enraged and sent forces to the holy city to punish the Jewish insurgents and re-established his authority over the region:

> Daniel 11:30
> …and [Antiochus IV] shall turn back and be enraged and take action against the holy covenant [Israel/Jerusalem]. He [Antiochus] shall turn back and pay attention [favor] to those who forsake the holy covenant [Hellenist Jews].

Antiochus and the Abomination of Desolation

As Daniel describes above, Antiochus affirmed the Jews who had embraced Hellenism but something inside him snapped against those Jews who did not. He employed a violent strategy to end the religious freedom that the Jews had enjoyed since his predecessor, Antiochus III, had granted them autonomy.

On December 6, 167 BC, Antiochus IV stopped the daily Jewish sacrifices to Yahweh in the temple and set up an altar to the Greek god Zeus to replace those sacrifices to his patron deity. This was called by Daniel the "abomination of desolation" that profaned the temple.

> Daniel 11:31
> Forces from him [Antiochus] shall appear and profane the temple and fortress, and shall take away the regular burnt offering. And they shall set up the **abomination that makes desolate**.

First Maccabees details the abominable desolation foretold by Daniel:

> 1 Maccabees 1:44–54 (LES)
> And the king [Antiochus IV Epiphanes] sent letters in the hands of messengers to Jerusalem and the cities of Judah, going after the customs of foreigners of the land, and to withhold burnt offerings and sacrifice and drink offering from the sanctuary and to profane Sabbaths and festivals, and to defile the sanctuary and holy things... And on the fifteenth day of Chislev, on the [one hundred and forty-fifth] year, **they built an abomination of desolation on the altar**.

First Maccabees gives more details later on what the pagan worship of the abomination of desolation included. But in short, the profaning involved not merely erecting a detestable idol, but suppressing Jewish circumcision, dietary laws and Sabbaths, while requiring sacrifices to Zeus with animals that the Jews considered unclean, such as pigs.

The Hellenist Jews flattered the king by participating in the profane abomination of these demands, but others did not. Many would not stop circumcising their sons, worshipping on Sabbaths or refraining from eating pork and other unclean animals. And they would certainly not take part in sacrifices to Zeus. The result was Antiochus's massive persecution and martyrdom of Jews described in the books of the Maccabees and earlier in this chapter. Daniel prophesied the suffering and martyrdom as a refining fire of holiness:

> Daniel 11:32–35
> He [Antiochus] shall seduce with flattery those who violate the covenant [Hellenist Jews], but the people who know their God [holy Jews] shall stand firm and take action [disobey Antiochus's decrees]. And the wise among the people shall make many understand, though for some days they shall stumble by sword and flame, by captivity and plunder. When they stumble, they shall receive a little help [from the Maccabean uprising] … and some of the wise shall stumble, so that they may be refined, purified, and made white, until the time of the end.

The family of Mattathias led by Judas Maccabeus, not only refused to obey but stood in violent resistance and built an army of defiance. Their war against the Seleucid king ended with temporary victory in 165 BC and Judas cleansed the Jerusalem temple of its abomination with a reinstatement of biblical sacrifices.[15]

Amazingly, Daniel foretold the amount of time this entire series of events would take: 2,300 days ("evenings and mornings"):

---

[15] 1 Maccabees 4:36-61; 2 Maccabees 10:1-9.

> Daniel 8:13–14
> "For how long is the vision concerning the regular burnt offering, the transgression that makes desolate, and the giving over of the sanctuary and host to be trampled underfoot?" And he said to me, "**For 2,300 evenings and mornings**. Then the sanctuary shall be restored to its rightful state."

2,300 days comes out to about six years and three months (the "evening and morning" phrase may refer to the fact that the daily sacrifice was actually performed in the evening and in the morning of each day). The description of the sanctuary and host being "trampled underfoot" does not refer to physical destruction but to the pagan forces' idolatrous, polluting presence of occupying that temple. Commentator Jay Rogers explains this fulfillment:

> This is the time period, exactly six-years and three-and-a-half-months, during which Antiochus occupied the city of Jerusalem. Although the Jews were oppressed for over six years under the tyranny of Antiochus, for the last three years of the occupation, the sacrifices ceased to be offered. The purifying of the Temple was not at the end of the sixth year, but not until the ninth month of the Jewish ecclesiastical year, Kislev (November/December), which is also the third month of the Jewish civil year.[16]

In all his defiance, the "little horn," Antiochus IV Epiphanes, did not thwart God's will. But he had tried. This incident marks Epiphanes as one of the most infamous of villains in Jewish history, indeed in Christian history since he would become a template for another future ruler who would set up a second abomination of desolation in the Jerusalem temple. A pattern of historical repetition.

---

[16] Jay Rogers, *In the Days of These Kings: The Book of Daniel in Preterist Perspective* (Clermont, FL: Media House International, 2017), 60.

The two places that Daniel describes this second abomination of desolation are in chapters 9 and 12:

> Daniel 9:26–27
> And the people of the prince who is to come shall destroy the city [Jerusalem] and the sanctuary. Its end shall come with a flood, and to the end there shall be war. **Desolations** are decreed. And he shall make a strong covenant with many for one week, and for half of the week he shall put an end to sacrifice and offering. And on the **wing of abominations shall come one who makes desolate**, until the decreed end is poured out on the **desolate**."

> Daniel 12:7–11
> When the shattering of the power of the holy people comes to an end all these things would be finished. I heard, but I did not understand. Then I said, "O my lord, what shall be the outcome of these things?" He said, "Go your way, Daniel, for the words are shut up and sealed **until the time of the end**…And from the time that the regular burnt offering is taken away and the **abomination that makes desolate** is set up, there shall be 1,290 days.

Though we read of similar terminology of "abomination of desolation" related to the holy people, temple, and city, we know that these prophesies are not about Antiochus Epiphanes but about a future abominator for several reasons. First, Antiochus Epiphanes only polluted the temple, but he did not destroy it. The second abominator would make the temple "desolate" (Daniel 9:27) *and* destroy both the city of Jerusalem and its temple (9:26). Antiochus did not destroy Jerusalem or the temple.

Second, the new abomination would occur at "the time of the end," "when the shattering of the power of the holy people comes to an end." The days of the Maccabees were not the end of anything in relation to God's timeline of history, for "the power" of the Jews did not come to an end, it kept on with the Maccabees' success. And that power would only be shattered for good when the Roman Beast would destroy the temple totally and permanently in the generation of Messiah Jesus.

Third, the return to the regular burnt offering in the days of Antiochus was 2,300 days (Daniel 8:14), not the 1,290 days spoken of here in Daniel 12:11.

So what we see then in Daniel are two different abominations of desolation that are called by the same epithet or nickname phrase because they share a pattern of behavior in relation to God's people and temple. They both invade God's holy temple, they both stop the daily sacrifice, and they both desolate the temple with idolatrous presence for a time. But the second one does worse in destroying both temple and city. At this point readers may want to engage in speculation as to who this new "prince" is and when he will arise in history. I have addressed that separate issue later in this book. For now, I want to continue with an exploration of the character of Antiochus IV Epiphanes as described by Scripture and history.

One aspect of that character is another repeating pattern of behavior in the kings of the "beastly" Gentile kingdoms: god-like pride. Arrogant ancient rulers always seem to want to overthrow God and take his place.

> Daniel 8:25
> And he [the little horn] shall even **rise up against the Prince of princes**, and he shall be broken—but by no human hand.

The phrase that Daniel uses to indicate the idolatrous arrogance of Gentile rulers involves derivations of "do as he wills." In Hebrew, do (*asah*) as he wills (*rason*). It carries the meaning of "doing what he pleases" as if the king was so great that like a god he could do whatever he wanted without resistance.

Daniel's first use of the phrase applies to King Cyrus the Great of Persia, who "*did as he willed* and became great. And there was no one who could rescue from his power" (Daniel 8:4). Daniel later describes Alexander the Great as "a mighty king who shall rule with great dominion and *do as he wills*" (11:3). After him comes Antiochus III the Great who would "*do as he wills* and none shall stand before him" (11:16).

The last king of which Daniel uses the phrase is one who would come "at the time of the end" of these kingdoms. This king would also "*do as he wills*" by "exalting himself and magnifying himself above every god and shall speak astonishing things against the God of gods" (Daniel 11:36). But this last willful king is not Antiochus IV Epiphanes because Antiochus was not the king *at the time of the end.* We will discuss who this king might be later. Let's stay with our focus on Epiphanes.

The willful king phrase takes an ironic twist when considered in its context of God, the king over all the earth, describing his sovereign predestination of their exact actions in history that would lead up to the finishing of the "transgression of Israel" against Yahweh (Daniel 11:36) through the coming of Messiah (Daniel 9:24). These kings all believed and behaved as if they were gods. But in the end, they were mere instruments in the true God's plans.

Antiochus Epiphanes is the only king in these chapters not referred to as "doing as he wills." Some English translations of Daniel 11:28 say that Antiochus "shall do as he will," but this is not in the Hebrew. It only says that he will act (asah) against the holy covenant. I.e., the first half of that phrase without the second willful component. Perhaps this is God's most demeaning and mocking gesture of all in avoiding even acknowledging the will of the "despicable" monster who profaned Yahweh's house with the abomination of desolation. He's just another axe in the hand of God chastising his people (Isaiah 10:5, 15).

That said, contextually Antiochus was certainly in the line of kings who acted with godlike pretensions. In another prophecy, Daniel details this blasphemous arrogance of Antiochus Epiphanes against Yahweh and his people and heavenly host.

> Daniel 8:9–11
> Out of one of them came a little horn [Antiochus Epiphanes], which grew exceedingly great toward the south, toward the east, and toward the glorious land [Israel]. It grew great, even to the host of heaven. And some of the host and some of the stars it threw down to the ground and trampled on them. It became great, even as great as the Prince of the host [Angel of Yahweh].

Could a mere human king actually be capable of casting angels of the heavenly host to the ground?[17] Could he really rival the greatness of the highest Prince of the heavenly host, the Angel of Yahweh himself?[18] In the context of the Scriptures, obviously not. Humans in the presence of real heavenly beings often tremble in deathly fright. These words are more likely a reflection of the little horn's blasphemous words of arrogance in the face of God. Something that history bears out and Daniel interprets just a few verses later as "in his own mind he shall become great.... He shall even rise up against the Prince of princes, and he shall be broken—but by no human hand" (8:25).

The epithet "Epiphanes" that Antiochus IV took meant "manifest god," a true affront to the only creator God Yahweh. This delusional surname expressed his tyrannical behavior and reflected a madness that eventually inspired a satirical twist of the word Epiphanes into "Epimanes," which meant "utterly mad" or "madman."[19]

Roman historian Polybius wrote of Antiochus fancying himself a god come down to men by wandering around town in royal garb or

---

[17] Stars are often symbols or representatives of elohim/gods/angels in the Bible and other Ancient Near Eastern literature, including Intertestamental Jewish literature. See my explanation of this literary symbolism in Brian Godawa When Watchers Ruled the Nations: Pagan Gods at War with Israel's God and the Spiritual World of the Bible (Texas: Warrior Poet Publishing, 2021), 29-37.

[18] There are two strong possibilities for understanding "The Prince of the host." He is either Michael the archangel or Yahweh himself, Jesus in preincarnate form. For Michael the archangel, see Brian Godawa, When Watchers Ruled the Nations: Pagan Gods at War with Israel's God and the Spiritual World of the Bible (Texas: Warrior Poet Publishing, 2021), 314-317. For the Angel of Yahweh as the Prince of the host, see Michael S. Heiser, *Angels: What the Bible Really Says about God's Heavenly Host* (Bellingham, WA: Lexham Press, 2018), 71–72.

[19] John Whitehorne, "Antiochus (Person)," in *The Anchor Yale Bible Dictionary*, ed. David Noel Freedman (New York: Doubleday, 1992), 270.

plebian disguise to discuss technical matters of the arts and crafts with goldsmiths and jewelers. He would engage in drinking bouts in the taverns with a couple of his trusted advisors, Heraclides and Timarchus of Miletus. He would bestow godlike excessive gifts of ointments, food, or money upon unwitting strangers in the streets, sometimes out of the blue, sometimes in response to overheard desires.[20]

But his unpredictable acts of caprice could have their sinister side as well for as historian Edwyn Bevan warns, beware the caresses of a panther. "He felt no difficulty in pleasantries with the man at whom he designed to strike."[21]

Roman historian Livy wrote that Antiochus would also adjudicate on the most trivial of legal matters as if divinely omniscient, then move on to petty common interactions with a rather short human patience. In Antioch, he spent extravagantly on religious and civic splendor. He began building the magnificent temple of Olympian Zeus, which was gilded with gold throughout, and splurged on Greek theaters and Roman gladiator arenas.[22]

Of all the Greek deities, Antiochus favored Zeus. Not only did the king build the Antioch temple dedicated to that Supreme Deity but had previously built a vast temple of "Zeus Olympius" in Athens. He also put the storm god's face on newly minted coins in his realm. There are some grounds to believe that Antiochus identified himself with Zeus as the king of the gods.[23]

Ironically, most scholars agree that Antiochus did not originally have a particular animosity toward the Jews. Despite this ostentatious display and public dedication to Zeus, Antiochus himself was quite without religion. As Barry explains:

---

[20] Polybius, *Histories* XXVI https://penelope.uchicago.edu/Thayer/E/Roman/Texts/Polybius/26*.html

[21] Edwyn Robert Bevan, *The House of Seleucus* (London, Edward Arnold Publishing, 1902), 129-130.

[22] Livy, Books XL-XLII With An English Translation, ed. Evan T. Sage and Alfred C. Schlesinger, *Ab Urbe Condita (Foster-Moore-Sage) English Text* (Medford, MA: Cambridge, Mass., Harvard University Press; London, William Heinemann, Ltd., 1938), 249–251.

[23] Bevan, *The House of Seleucus*, 150.

> His devotion to the worship of Zeus was but part of his idea that there be, instead of divers local and tribal faiths, a formal state religion, to become a powerful unifying factor, as a means of giving securer basis of solidarity to his empire.[24]

The king's imposition of Hellenism was that attempt to unify the empire through the transcendence of deity and religion. In a sense, he was playing with fire, the fire of true believers that he could not understand.

The death of Antiochus Epiphanes has more than one narrative in the books of the Maccabees. In 1 Maccabees 6, the Seleucid king is in Persia unsuccessfully seeking to plunder the city of Elymais to increase his waning wealth. A messenger tells Antiochus of Lysias's defeat to Judas Maccabeus in the battle of Beth-Zur and the subsequent cleansing of the temple, whereupon the king becomes physically sick with disappointment. A sickness that he believed would kill him. Pondering his deathbed, he painfully regrets his poor treatment of the Jews but doesn't repent so much as suffer spiritual punishment for his choices. He then appoints a regent over his young son until he is of age to reign. Then Antiochus dies. The writer wants to console himself that the king experiences some kind of justice in this world before he dies.

In 2 Maccabees 9, a different and more interesting tale is told with no less a religious agenda and a far greater hunger for earthly judgment. Antiochus is in Persepolis, Persia, seeking to rob its temples and assert control. He fails and retreats to Ecbatana near Babylonia, where he receives a message of Seleucid defeats by the Maccabees but *before* the temple's cleansing has occurred.

Antiochus becomes so angry he leaves for Jerusalem, shouting in arrogance, "When I get there, I will make Jerusalem a cemetery of Jews" (9:4). We are then told that God in his providential retribution strikes the king with "a pain in his bowels, for which there was no relief, and with

[24] Phillips Barry, "Antiochus IV, Epiphanes," *Journal of Biblical Literature*, Vol. 29, No. 2 (1910), pp. 126-138

sharp internal tortures—and that very justly, for he had tortured the bowels of others with many and strange inflictions" (9:5-6). This does not deter Antiochus from his raging path. In fact, he tells his chariot driver to go faster. Unfortunately, the king falls out of the vehicle, and "the fall was so hard as to torture every limb of his body" (9:7).

In a verbose display of literary poetic justice, the writer mocks the king's epithet of "god manifest" by saying that he who once thought he had the "power of God manifest to all" was now "swarmed with worms" with an "intolerable stench" from the "rotting of his flesh." The storyteller really wants Antiochus to suffer deeply in this life for the pain he has caused as otherwise the Jewish suffering would seem without just recompense.

But Antiochus is enlightened and expresses his regret, not unlike King Nebuchadnezzar's revelation in the wild: "It is right to be subject to God; mortals should not think that they are equal to God" (9:12). Still, the writer does not want Antiochus to have the full release of forgiveness so he reminds us that even though the king made a vow to God to free the Jews from persecution and return the wealth he had stolen from the temple, "the Lord would no longer have mercy on him" (9:13).

Antiochus then appointed his son to take the throne. The writer concludes, "So the murderer and blasphemer, having endured the more intense suffering, such as he had inflicted on others, came to the end of his life by a most pitiable fate, among the mountains in a strange land" (9:28).

Abominable. Miserable. His flesh rotting. His bowels swollen with worms. His suffering unabated. In summary, the reader of 2 Maccabees can safely say of Antiochus Epiphanes, "Good riddance."

Partial or Dual Fulfillment?

At this point, some Bible prophecy speculators will concede that the little horn and abomination of desolation in Daniel 8 and 11 are fulfilled in Antiochus Epiphanes in 168-165 BC. But they argue that he is only a "partial fulfillment" of this prophecy. That there is still an abomination of desolation in our future which will also fulfill these prophecies in an ultimate sense. Put another way, they believe there is a short-term fulfillment in Antiochus and a long-term fulfillment in another ruler yet to come. Antiochus then becomes only a type of fulfillment but not the final one. He is either a "partial fulfillment" or one of dual or multiple fulfillments of the same prophecy. These speculators claim the prophecies are *really* pointing toward someone else in our future. Sometimes they will even argue that there are many "abominations of desolation" and "little horns" in history (Hitler, Mussolini, Stalin, etc.) that point toward this ultimate abomination of desolation.

This is a dangerous, unbiblical hermeneutic.

Those who hold this view have not thought through what they are really arguing for. Their view ultimately reduces Bible prophecy to subjective arbitrary putty that can be pressed into any shape according to the interpreter's personal subjective tastes. The result is that Bible prophecy can fit whatever schema any interpreter can make it fit. Let's look at how this plays out.

First, what does "partial fulfillment" even mean? Does that mean Antiochus only fulfilled some of the prophecies but not all of them? That would be empirically false. I have shown how that little horn, the Seleucid king, and his abominable idol fulfilled *all the prophecies* related to the abomination of desolation in Daniel 8 and 11. To say that he only partially fulfilled those prophecies is to deny the historical facts.

If by "partial" the interpreter means that it is only one of two or more fulfillments of the same prophecy, then they still have the problem of imposing their preconceived bias upon the text. Where in the Bible does it say these prophecies are about anything other than the singular historic events they predict? Nowhere. It either fulfills the prophecy or it does not. If it fulfills the prophecy, where does the prophet say there will be others? To see the historic fulfillment of these prophesies and declare two or more fulfillments of one prophecy is to claim a mystical or secret knowledge of the "real meaning" of the prophecy that is not apparent in the text. This would reduce prophecy to the arbitrary whim of every private interpretation.

Another problem with partial, dual, or multiple fulfillments is that Daniel's prophecies are specifically rooted in historical events that explicitly point to one time period of history that ended in Messiah in the first century AD. Consider the fact that Daniel's dream interpretation in Daniel 2 is all about the arrival of Messiah, who brings the Kingdom of God "in the days of these kings" (2:44). What kings? Daniel explains that Nebuchadnezzar's dream of the metallic statue symbolically represented four kingdoms in succession—the Babylonians, the Medo-Persians, the Greeks, and the Romans (2:36-43). These are exactly the kingdoms that we see in past history.

Daniel then says that the Messiah would bring his kingdom in the days of the last kingdom, that of Rome (2:34, 44-45). From that day forward, the Messiah's kingdom would grow to overcome all the other kingdoms (2:44-45). This all happened in history just as Daniel predicted. The Medo-Persians conquered the Babylonians, the Macedonian Greek king Alexander the Great conquered Media-Persia, and then ancient Rome eventually filled the power vacuum left by Alexander's weakened kingdom.

Some futurists try to deny the contiguous history in the prophecy, claiming that it is not about the first coming of Jesus but his second coming. They believe that the Roman kingdom of iron mixed with clay is not the ancient Roman kingdom into which Jesus came but that Daniel skips right over the coming of Messiah, jumping thousands of years later to his second coming. The Roman empire in the prophecy then becomes a "rebuilt Roman empire" in our future, not the ancient Roman empire that came right after the Greek empire in actual history.

This makes no sense and doesn't fit the prophecy. Why would Daniel, whose entire purpose is to predict the coming of Messiah after all these Gentile kingdoms, just ignore that first coming and jump thousands of years later to a second coming? It would turn the first coming into an inconsequential event.

There is nowhere in the text that says there is a gap of thousands of years before the last kingdom. On the contrary, they are successive kingdoms which happen to match history perfectly. Ancient Rome came after ancient Greece just as Nebuchadnezzar's dream predicted. Messiah came during that kingdom and brought it all down just a few centuries after his arrival—just as the "rock cut without hands" in the prophecy struck the statue at the Roman feet, demolishing it.

The futurist prejudice is so blinding it will ignore the prophecy of the first coming of Messiah to maintain its presumed scenario for the future. Such interpretation skips over the obvious fulfillment and inserts a two-plus-thousand-year gap that is not in the text to push the last kingdom into the future. The futurist engages in revising the Bible itself to keep their eschatological system from collapsing into absurdity.

To reinforce the interpretation that Daniel is speaking of the four kingdoms of our past history, the rest of his book chronicles that history in more detail through other visions. Daniel has another vision under the Babylonian king Belshazzar that zooms in on the Medo-Perisan kingdom and then the Greek kingdom to come (Daniel 8). He depicts Alexander the Great as a mighty goat that overcomes a ram symbolizing Medo-Persia. This actually happened. Then in 8:9-14, he explains Antiochus Epiphanes and his abomination of desolation coming out of that Greek kingdom as the little horn we exegeted earlier.

In Daniel 10, we read about the spiritual principality of Persia who will soon be battling the principality of Greece just as the Greek kingdom of Alexander the Great eventually took over Persia in history. Then in Daniel 11, we get a dizzying series of wars between the "kings of the north" and the "kings of the south," which refer to the Syrian Wars between the Greek Seleucids and Ptolemies after Alexander (see my chart at the end of this book about fulfillment of Daniel 11 in the lead-up to and including the Syrian Wars of the second century BC).

Antiochus Epiphanes appears in 11:20 as the final willful king of that series who brings his abomination of desolation.

After Antiochus comes the final king at the time of the end and the events of Daniel 12 that are during the days of ancient Rome. All this narrative requires more exegesis than this small booklet can offer.[25] But I think I have demonstrated clearly enough from Daniel's context from beginning to end is all about the four Gentile kingdoms that would oppress Israel until Messiah came. And that's what biblical history is, a history of Israel, not the Gentile world.

Over and over again, the book of Daniel spells out prophetic and symbolic references to the Babylonians, the Medo-Persians, the Greeks (especially the Seleucids and Ptolemies), and then the Romans. Daniel's context is so clearly about Israel's past history until Messiah that to say it is also symbolic of a future fulfillment is to engage in interpretive violence against the text. It is wrenching prophecies out of their full context in the book and arbitrarily applying them to some speculative future that the interpreter can only speculate.

This brings me to another problem with this futurist interpretive catastrophe. Some will argue that there is precedent for dual fulfillment claims in Daniel by pointing to Messianic prophecies that seem to have a short-term fulfillment in the Old Testament and a long-term fulfillment in the New Testament in Jesus. For instance, they will claim that prophecies like Isaiah 7 about the virgin birth of Messiah apply to a local referent. God is speaking to king Ahaz and telling him that a young maiden in his presence would have a child who would not be fully grown before King Rezin of Damascus and "the son of Remaliah" of Israel would find their land deserted.[26] New Testament writers then tell us that these prophecies also apply to Jesus as the Messiah (Matthew 1:22-23).

---

[25] For more details on Daniel's prophecies of history see my podcast series, "Daniel and End Times Prophecy": https://www.youtube.com/playlist?list=PL5TyMLcYh4AOPA4WGoSAr9rSxUEMgv2hC

[26] Gene M. Tucker, "The Book of Isaiah 1–39," in *New Interpreter's Bible*, ed. Leander E. Keck, vol. 6 (Nashville: Abingdon Press, 1994–2004), 111.

This kind of dual fulfillment in messianic prophecy is another subject too complex to address here. But for the sake of argument, I will assume it is true that some Old Testament prophecies pointing to Jesus as Messiah may also have a local referent in Old Testament history. Here is the problem for the futurist. The ones who have made the dual-fulfillment claim regarding Messianic prophecies are New Testament apostles, who were the New Testament equivalent of the Old Testament prophets. They spoke for God, and their writings became Scripture. Jesus had actually invested them with his authority as his representatives (John 14:26), his ultimate authorities on earth (1 Corinthians 12:28).

For a Christian to look at the New Testament apostles and to conclude that we now have the same authority to claim dual fulfillments of prophecies *that the apostles did not claim* is to place ourselves and our subjective interpretations in the place of apostolic authority or prophets of God.[27] One would be saying, "I have new revelation from God that tells me that the prophecies of Daniel, though fulfilled in the past history of the four Gentile kingdoms, *also* have a future fulfillment to come." That claim by definition is "new revelation" because in the text, Daniel makes no explicit expectation of dual fulfillment. That is bringing a new interpretation that extends beyond what the prophecy actually predicts and fulfills. It is adding to the written Word of God.

I don't know any Christian who would want to make such an explicit claim. But that is exactly what one is doing when one says, "I can do what the apostles did. I can declare dual fulfillments even where the text does not." Only a bona fide prophet of God can claim to speak for God and therefore make connections such as "out of Egypt I called my Son" is also about Jesus (Hosea 11:1; Matthew 2:15). We do not have the right to do what the apostles and prophets of God did in exegeting dual fulfillments, if that is in fact what they did.

---

27 The New Testament spiritual gift of prophecy is not the same as Old Testament prophets. The apostles are.

But the implications are far worse. If one claims that prophecies have dual or multiple fulfillments, then every prophecy can be so interpreted. That would mean there could be another Son of David born in Bethlehem of a virgin who would take the sins of the world upon himself. Outrageous! Yes, but as soon as you say you cannot do that, you have put an arbitrary restriction that contradicts your original interpreting principle. You have said prophecies can have dual fulfillments, just not *those* prophecies. But what restricts you? And where do you stop? It's arbitrary. If your standard is that prophecies can have dual fulfillments, that means messianic prophecies can too. And why not triple fulfillments? Or more?

Well, you may say, Jesus already came and died for our sins once and for all, so that can't happen again. Precisely. Once a prophecy is fulfilled, there is no "dual fulfillment" or you reduce it to subjective putty that is hostage to the whims of interpreters and makes us all prophets of God. If I can find any kind of similarity or connection between arbitrary words in the Old Testament and something in today's world, I have claimed a new revelation of God's Word.

This is not so absurd or unrealistic as it sounds. There are religious "Christian" writers and speakers today who interpret the Bible this way, taking Scriptures out of context and finding mystical new fulfillments in the present time. I have read one of them claim that historical events depicted in the Old Testament, such as the story of Jezebel and Elijah, are prophecy "templates" for events being fulfilled in our day in America. With the wave of an interpretive wand, the historical Old Testament account has been turned into prophecies for today without any justification from Scripture whatsoever. Not analogies, actual prophecies. And this man claims it is revelation from the Holy Spirit.

By that claim, his writing of these so-called prophecies should be considered Scripture. He probably wouldn't claim that, but it is the logical conclusion of his premises. If God is giving him new revelation that some historical story in the Old Testament is now a prophecy, then he should logically conclude that his "revelation" is the Word of God and should be written down as scripture. This is an obvious blasphemy in claiming new revelation after apostolic authority has passed away. This is not some obscure preacher in a small church somewhere. This is a mega-bestselling "teacher," and untold hundreds of thousands of Christians are following his delusion of false prophecies.

But I hope you can see how multiple fulfillments of prophecy becomes an arbitrary interpretive rule that results in every person speaking as a prophet through private interpretation of Scripture taken out of context. If prophecy has multiple fulfillments, why can't I claim that Abraham Lincoln's emancipation of the slaves is a "partial fulfillment" of Isaiah 6:1 of "proclaiming liberty to the captives," or that the lion with eagle wings in Daniel's vision about Babylon is a dual prophecy about America because the eagle is our national bird and we are like a powerful lion in the world. All analogies become prophecies. The possible interpretations are literally endless, reducing Bible prophecies into putty that a million interpretations can shape, making a million prophets of God. In the dual- or multiple-fulfillment view, prophecy is reduced to nonsense that can be applied to anything with which the interpreter can find a similarity. It is more like a vision about Babel.

Chapter 4
The Gods

The reader of Chronicles of the Watchers should be familiar with the biblical idea of the gods or spiritual principalities and powers in heaven over human rulers and powers on earth. I have written extensively of this aspect of biblical theology in previous books.[1] But a review of that worldview is helpful as I lay the groundwork for an examination of the Greek and Roman gods that appear in the *Judah Maccabee* novels.

Gods in the Bible

To begin with, Christians consider themselves monotheists. They believe there is only one God. Some believe that this means that other gods do not exist in the real world but are instead pure constructs of human imagination. They will claim that the Bible itself says this in its most pertinent passage, the Shema of Israel:

> Deuteronomy 6:4
> "Hear, O Israel: The LORD our God, the LORD is one."

But there is a subtle issue at play here. To say "our God is one" is to say that we worship one God. But it has nothing to say about the reality of other gods who are being rejected.

> Deuteronomy 10:17
> For the LORD your God is God of gods and Lord of lords,
> the great, the mighty, and the awesome God.

---

[1] Brian Godawa, *When Giants Were Upon the Earth: The Watchers, the Nephilim, and the Biblical Cosmic War of the Seed*, (Los Angeles: Embedded Pictures Publishing, 2014); Brian Godawa, *When Watchers Ruled the Nations: Pagan Gods at War with Israel's God and the Spiritual World of the Bible* (Allen, TX: Warrior Poet Publishing, 2014).

There is something going on here. God is the "God of gods?" Well, if "Lord of lords" does not negate the existence of other lords, but merely subordinates them to Yahweh, then "God of gods" can certainly be a reiteration of the same idea of subordination.

But then in many other places, the Bible appears to say that other gods do not exist. Or do they? When Moses writes about the Israelites worshipping the gods of Canaan, he calls those gods "demons which are not God."

> Deuteronomy 32:17 (NIV84)
> They sacrificed to **demons, which are not God—gods** they had not known, **gods that recently appeared, gods** your fathers did not fear.[2]

But there are problems here, too, because if the text describes Canaanite gods as demons, then according to God's own words, they possess an ontological reality. And there are many other Bible passages that do speak of there being other gods—supernatural or spiritual entities—who exist in addition to Yahweh. Here are just a few:

> Psalm 82:1–8
> God has taken his place in the divine council;
> in the midst of **the gods** he holds judgment:
> "How long will you judge unjustly
> and show partiality to the wicked?..."
> "I said, '**You are gods**,
> sons of the Most High, all of you…'"

> Psalm 29:1
> Ascribe to the LORD, **O gods**, ascribe to the LORD glory
> and strength.

[2] I use the NIV84 translation here because the ESV poorly translates this passage. The ESV says, "They sacrificed to demons that were no gods..." which gives the false impression that the gods are not gods, rather than simply stating that the gods (*elohim*) are not the Creator God, who is also referred to as *Elohim*, and who they were supposed to worship exclusively. Demons are real beings, so if one believed that the word "god" could only be used of real beings, then the verse would be contradictory, because demons are real beings.

> Deuteronomy 32:43
> "Rejoice with him, O heavens; **bow down to him, all gods**..."

So, we see that on the one hand, the Bible says that Yahweh is one God. And on the other hand, it says that there are other spiritual beings called "gods," that Yahweh himself calls "gods" (Psalm 82:6), that do exist in reality and outside of the imagination of humans.

Is this polytheism? Does this mean that the Bible contradicts itself? By no means! Understanding the solution to this apparent discrepancy begins in uncovering the ancient Hebrew language and cultural context behind the word for "gods," which is *elohim*.

The problem is that when we Westerners see the Hebrew word translated "god" (*elohim*) we import all kinds of meaning into the word that the Hebrews did not. We assume that every instance of *elohim* comprises the sole biblical category of an all-knowing, all-powerful, all-present Creator. In other words, we assume an *elohim* possesses the character traits of a single being, Yahweh. But the Bible does not assume those traits in its definition of god/*elohim*.

Elohim is a plural term in Hebrew. But it could be used of a singular entity, such as Yahweh, in Deuteronomy 6:4 above. Or it could be used of the pantheon of Canaanite deities, as in Deuteronomy 32:17 above. Or it could be used of angels of God's divine council who surround his throne, as in Psalm 82 above.

So, how is it that the same word "god," used of Yahweh our Creator, could be used in the Bible of other creatures who are not Yahweh? What we see is that the biblical definition of gods/*elohim* involves multiple beings that all have one thing in common, from Yahweh to heavenly host: they all exist and operate within the spiritual realm. To say that something is a god in the Bible is not to say that it is omnipotent or infinite or even a Creator. It is merely to refer to its residence in the heavenly realm as opposed to human residence in the earthly realm.

This is why Yahweh is called "God of gods." It does not mean that he is God of imaginary gods. That would not make sense. What it means is that he is the ultimate spiritual being of all spiritual beings. This is not polytheism. But it is also not absolute monotheism that denies the existence of other divine beings. Unfortunately, our modern Western worldview has been prejudiced by an absolute monotheism that there is only one god/*elohim* who exists: Yahweh. No other gods exist.

As tempting as it is to lean toward this absolutism, it is not biblical. In the Bible, the word *god* has a looser and broader definition than our modern Western definition. I would argue that we should adjust our language to match the Bible, not the other way around.

The Apostle Paul helps clarify this definition in 1 Corinthians, where he draws upon the Shema and Deuteronomy 32:17 above to explain pagan gods as in one sense having no power, and in another sense, having real existence with whatever power we allow them in our lives. Regarding the debate over eating food sacrificed to idols he says this:

> 1 Corinthians 8:4–6 (NKJV)
> Therefore concerning the eating of things offered to idols, we know that an idol is nothing in the world, and that there is no other God but one. For even if there are so-called gods, whether in heaven or on earth (as there are many gods and many lords), yet **for us there is one God**, the Father, of whom are all things.

On the one hand, it may look as if Paul is saying that other gods do not exist. But he is not. He is referring to idols, or images of gods, used in ritual sacrifice, not the gods they represent (Paul will refer to those later). He is saying that those images are nothing in the cosmos of the Christian. When he says that "for us" there is one God, he is clarifying the Shema as being the standard for God's people in the midst of pagan worshippers of other gods. He does not deny the existence of other gods because just one verse later he says explicitly, "there are so-called gods" in heaven. And his language of "even if" and "so-called" does not make those gods mere figments of others' imagination, but rather makes them shrink to nothing *compared with* Yahweh. That's the context. He stresses this comparative worth (not existence) by addressing the ranked system, not the beings ("for us" as opposed to "for them").

And here is the point: though the idols are "nothing," the spiritual beings they represent (behind them) are real. Again, this is not polytheism as the modern absolute monotheist defines it. Because Paul later in the letter explains that those pagan gods behind the earthly images (idols) *are really demons*:

> 1 Corinthians 10:18–21
> Consider the people of Israel: are not those who eat the sacrifices participants in the altar? What do I imply then? That food offered to idols is anything, or that an idol is anything? No, I imply that what pagans sacrifice **they offer to demons and not to God**. I do not want you to be **participants with demons**. You cannot drink the cup of the Lord and the **cup of demons**. You cannot partake of the table of the Lord and the **table of demons**.

Paul is saying that the altars you worship at, whether the Lord's Supper or pagan sacrifices, constitute participation with the spiritual entities behind those rituals. Once again, he clarifies that the earthly idol/image is nothing, but that the spiritual god *behind the idol* is real, and pagan gods are demons. Demons are not nothing. Demons do not exist solely in men's imaginations. Demons, called gods in the Bible, are real spiritual beings.

This reference to sacrificing to demons should bring to mind a previous verse we already quoted above:

> Deuteronomy 32:17 (NIV84)
> They sacrificed to demons, **which are not God—gods** they had not known, **gods that recently appeared, gods** your fathers did not fear.

Paul is alluding to this Old Testament verse about demon gods in his argument to the Corinthians. He is explaining that both Old and New Testaments affirm that pagan gods are not "non-existent," they are not simply figments of our imagination. They have real spiritual, demonic reality behind them.

But it gets even more interesting because the word for *demon* in the New Testament had become an assumed negative reference to the evil spiritual realm. But the original Greek word he was using (*daimon*) was not considered as such in the Greco-Roman world to whom he was speaking. And the Hebrew word for *demon* in the Old Testament was *sheddim*, which had a more nuanced meaning more in line with the ancient Greek. Let's take a look at that nuance.

Gods of the Nations

The Greek word Paul used for demon originally had a fuller meaning in the ancient world than merely an evil spirit who possessed sinners. The *Theological Dictionary of the New Testament* explains that *demon* in the Hellenistic literature was first used to denote *gods*, then lesser deities, and finally "protective deities" watching over men. In this worldview, they could be either good or evil spiritual entities.[3]

> Not until post-Exilic times in intertestamental literature, with the rise of dualism and the concept of the Devil, did the word [*daimon*] begin to display the meaning 'evil demon in league with the Devil' and take on an entirely negative connotation… Christian writers use it almost exclusively in this later sense. The related term [*daimonion*] in the classical period meant similarly 'the divine power' or 'the Divinity'. It could also mean the

[3] Werner Foerster, "Δαίμων, Δαιμόνιον, Δαιμονίζομαι, Δαιμονιώδης, Δεισιδαίμων, Δεισιδαιμονία," in *Theological Dictionary of the New Testament*, ed. Gerhard Kittel, Geoffrey W. Bromiley, and Gerhard Friedrich (Grand Rapids, MI: Eerdmans, 1964), 2–3.

> class of lower divine beings 'between gods and mortals' who mediated between the human and divine spheres.[4]

Michael Heiser explains that the Hebrew *sheddim* was the equivalent of the Greek *daimon.*

> This rarely used term (Deut 32:17; Psa 106:37) comes from the Akkadian *shedu*. In the ancient Near East, the term *shedu* was neutral; it could speak of a good or malevolent spirit being. These Akkadian figures were often cast as guardians or protective entities, though the term was also used to describe the life force of a person. In the context of Deuteronomy 32:17, *shedim* were *elohim*—spirit beings guarding foreign territory—who must not be worshiped.[5]

This concept of guardian gods/*elohim* over territories or earthly authorities has its place in the Bible as well. Evidently, at the Tower of Babel, when Yahweh divided the people into nations with different tongues, he placed those "Gentile" nations under the authority of supernatural beings called "Sons of God" or *bene Elohim*, while keeping the people of Israel as his own allotment:

> Deuteronomy 32:8–9
> When the Most High gave to the nations their inheritance, when he divided mankind, he fixed the borders of the peoples according to the number of the sons of God. But the LORD's portion is his people, Jacob his allotted heritage.

Paul referred to this ancient allotment of territories as well. While he only speaks of the human nations, the language certainly alludes to the Deuteronomy 32 worldview of allotted boundaries/borders.

---

4 G. J. Riley, "Demon," in *Dictionary of Deities and Demons in the Bible*, ed. Karel van der Toorn, Bob Becking, and Pieter W. van der Horst (Leiden; Boston; Köln; Grand Rapids, MI; Cambridge: Brill; Eerdmans, 1999), 235.

5 Michael S. Heiser, *The Unseen Realm: Recovering the Supernatural Worldview of the Bible*, First Edition (Bellingham, WA: Lexham Press, 2015), 33.

> Acts 17:26
> And he made from one man every nation of mankind to live on all the face of the earth, having determined allotted periods and the boundaries of their dwelling place…

Elsewhere I have done extensive exegesis of the term *Sons of God* to show that they are originally divine angelic beings who surround God's throne in heaven (Job 1:6; 2:1; 38:7) and are part of his divine council of gods (Psalm 82:1, 6; 89:5-8).[6] Some of these *elohim*/gods/Sons of God had rebelled against Yahweh and sought to corrupt the human race before the Flood (Genesis 6:1-4). Then at Babel, God allotted earthly territories, or Gentile nations to some Sons of God who were expected to rule over them (Deuteronomy 32:8-9). Those territorial spirits failed to rule justly and engaged in wickedness, so God promised to judge them and ultimately disinherit them or take back their allotted territories (Psalm 82). This is the redemption of the Gentile nations that represents the Gospel of Jesus Christ.

The ancient understanding was that spiritual principalities and powers ruled over earthly authorities and kingdoms. So if there was a war on earth, there was a war in heaven. If spiritual powers fell, their earthly powers fell with them. We see this language in the description of the spiritual principalities of Persia, Greece, and Israel in battle as the earthly kings of Persia and Greece fought for their control over Israel in Daniel 10. Most scholars agree that the Hebrew word for "prince" (*sar*) in Daniel 10 refers to spiritual beings:

> Daniel 10:13, 20-21
> [The spiritual prince said to Daniel:] The [spiritual] prince of the kingdom of Persia withstood me twenty-one days, but Michael, one of the chief princes [archangel], came to help me, for I was left there with the kings of Persia…

---

[6] Brian Godawa, *When Giants Were Upon the Earth: The Watchers, the Nephilim, and the Biblical Cosmic War of the Seed*, (Los Angeles: Embedded Pictures Publishing, 2014); Brian Godawa, *When Watchers Ruled the Nations: Pagan Gods at War with Israel's God and the Spiritual World of the Bible* (Allen, TX: Warrior Poet Publishing, 2014).

> Then he said, "But now I will return to fight against the prince of Persia; and when I go out, behold, the prince of Greece will come. But I will tell you what is inscribed in the book of truth: there is none who contends by my side against these except Michael, your prince.

We also see this heaven-and-earth link in the heavenly armies at war influencing the earthly armies of Syria and Israel during Elisha's day.

> 2 Kings 6:17–18
> Then Elisha prayed and said, "O LORD, please open his eyes that he may see." So the LORD opened the eyes of the young man, and he saw, and behold, the mountain was full of horses and chariots of fire all around Elisha.

In the Bible, these supernatural principalities over nations, cities, or peoples are described as heavenly host, which had two meanings at the same time. It referred to those angelic beings around Yahweh's throne who also were likened to the celestial beings of the sun, moon, and stars (Deuteronomy 4:19-20).[7] So, when a nation or authority was defeated, the historical event was described as a cosmic collapse of falling stars and sun going dark. When God judges earthly kings, he also judges the heavenly host of spiritual powers over them.[8]

> Isaiah 24:21–22
> On that day the LORD will punish the **host of heaven**, in heaven, and **the kings of the earth,** on the earth.

Paul's language in the New Testament reaffirms this motif of spiritual "rulers," "powers," and "authorities" in heavenly places over their earthly equivalents as he describes the spiritual warfare they too

---

[7] See also parallelism in Psalm 148:2-3, Job 38:7, and Daniel 8:10-11.

[8] See also: the fall of Sisera and his armies - Judges 5:19-20; the fall of Babylon to the Medes (539 BC) - Isaiah 13:9-11; the fall of Edom (587 BC) - Isaiah 34:4-5; the fall of Egypt to Babylon (580 BC) - Ezekiel 32:7-8, 11. For more details on collapsing universe symbolism, see my *End Times Bible Prophecy: It's Not What They Told You* (Allen, TX: Warrior Poet Publishing, 2021).

had faced (Ephesians 6:12).[9] This is the biblical basis for my depiction of the pagan gods of Greece and Rome as real spiritual beings. They are the "Watchers" or the spiritual powers that were appointed over the Gentile nations and they ruled unjustly, wickedly usurping Yahweh's place as the one God to whom humans owe worship. To dig deeper into these biblical concepts, see my *Psalm 82: The Divine Council of the Gods, the Judgment of the Watchers and the Inheritance of the Nations.*

Sex of the Gods

One other note of importance is that the reader of all my Chronicles series will notice that I depict the original source's pagan deities in the female as well as male sex. Ba'al is a male deity, Anat is a female deity. Zeus is male, his wife Hera is female. Upon closer inspection, however, the female deities are revealed to be male Watchers masquerading as females. They refashion their flesh or use occultism to manipulate their visible presentation as female.

The reason why I have done this is because the Bible speaks of the Divine Council members, Sons of God/Watchers, and spiritual angels as being exclusively male in their sex, names, and pronouns, but it does not explain why. It is therefore reasonable to conclude that there are no female *elohim*.

But this is an argument from silence. An argument from silence is the conclusion that something does not exist because it is not spoken of in the text. The problem with this view is that there are a lot of things not spoken of in the Bible that *do* exist. For example, the name of Lot's wife, platypuses, and China. But that does not mean that Lot's wife did not have a name or that there are no platypuses or a country of China. So, because this is an argument from silence, it would be extra-biblical speculation to suggest that there are female Watchers or angels, but it would not necessarily be anti-biblical heresy.

---

9 See also Ephesians 1:20-21; 2:2; 3:10.

The caveat to the argument from silence is that it is reversible. Just because something is not discussed does not mean it exists and is being hidden or ignored. Sometimes silence *is* a deliberate expression of existential reality or theological purpose. In this case, we can only speculate why, but I have adopted the biblical silence as deliberate and purposeful and therefore I have suggested that any female presentation of fallen Sons of God/Watchers are façades or illusive disguises that hide the true male sexual identity of the beings.

The New Testament claims that the *satan* and his ilk can masquerade as angels of light (2 Corinthians 11:14), which means they can disguise their identities for nefarious purposes. So it is certainly reasonable to conclude that they can disguise their sexual identity as well.

The one passage some people point to as depicting female angels is Zechariah 5:9-11, which describes a vision a male angel gives Zechariah regarding the exile into Babylon:

> Zechariah 5:9-11
> Then I lifted my eyes and saw, and behold, two women coming forward! The wind was in their wings. They had wings like the wings of a stork, and they lifted up the basket between earth and heaven. Then I said to the angel who talked with me, "Where are they taking the basket?" He said to me, "To the land of Shinar, to build a house for it. And when this is prepared, they will set the basket down there on its base."

Some think that because these women have wings, they must be angels. But angels are never described as having wings in the Bible. Seraphim and cherubim are described as having wings, but not angels (Hebrew: *malakim*). Also, the women are not described as angels in the vision. In contrast, the angel with Zechariah *is* described as an angel—and with male pronouns.

This is a symbolic vision describing Yahweh taking away a disobedient Israel into exile in Babylon for her sins to be purged. The wings of the stork on the women are wings of unclean birds, symbolizing Israel's uncleanness. Angels of God would not have unclean wings. The land of Shinar is Mesopotamia, the land of Babylon, where Israel was in exile. The "house" Yahweh says is their new residence he built for them is most likely the ziggurat that represented the house of the gods of Babylon, who were to become the new lords over Israel's prison house punishment.[10]

The winged women are not angels. They are prophetic symbols of exilic judgment upon the nation of Israel.

Gods of the Greeks

Since we are exploring the Hellenistic time period of the Maccabees, it is helpful to know that the Greeks too believed in some gods as heavenly rulers placed in authority over earthly rulers and authorities. And they called those heavenly rulers *demons* (*daimon* in the Greek). Remember, to the Greek mind, demons were not necessarily evil, they were spiritual powers who could be either good or evil. And those ruling powers (*sheddim*) are what Moses referred to in Deuteronomy 32:17 as the pagan gods that resided over the land of Canaan.

The Hellenistic world had drunk deeply from the well of the ancient Greek philosopher Plato. It is no surprise then to find that he too wrote about the "allotment" of nations and territories to ruling spiritual powers (*daimon*/*daemons*). I quote extensively here to show the Greek affinity with the Deuteronomy worldview:

---

[10] See Mark J. Boda, *The Book of Zechariah*, ed. R. K. Harrison and Robert L. Hubbard Jr., The New International Commentary on the Old Testament (Grand Rapids, MI; Cambridge, UK.: William B. Eerdmans Publishing Company, 2016), 351–355.

> Plato, *Laws* 4.713, 738
> Cronos [the creator god]...appointed as kings and rulers for our cities, not men, but beings of a race that was nobler and more divine, namely, **daemons**...In like manner the God, in his love for humanity, set over us at that time the nobler race of **daemons** who, with much comfort to themselves and much to us, took charge of us and furnished peace and modesty and orderliness and justice without stint, and thus made the tribes of men free from feud and happy...to each section he should **assign a god or daemon**, or at the least a hero; and in the **distribution of the land** he should assign first to these **divinities choice domains** with all that pertains to them.[11]

> Plato, *Critias* 109b-c
> Once upon a time the gods were taking over **by lot the whole earth according to its regions**... So by just **allotments** they received each one his own, and they settled their countries... and thus they drove and steered all the mortal kind. Now in other regions others of **the gods had their allotments** and ordered the affairs.[12]

Now just because Greeks or any other pagan culture believed in territorial powers called *daemons* does not mean those beings exist. But if we are wondering what Jews meant when they discussed territorial spiritual powers and we see that other pagan cultures have similar beliefs, we can at least have a more accurate context of what the Jews meant by the term rather than imposing our own modern context.

Interestingly, there has been a theory since the days of Augustine that Plato may have drawn ideas from Moses. Plato's writings reveal concepts of the Creator that align with the Bible more than the Greek worldview, such as God's eternal nature and self-existence, as well as

---

[11] Plato, *Plato in Twelve Volumes & 11* Translated by R.G. Bury., vol. 10 (Medford, MA: Cambridge, MA: Harvard University Press; London: William Heinemann Ltd., 1967 & 1968).

[12] Plato, *Plato in Twelve Volumes* Translated by W.R.M. Lamb., vol. 9 (Medford, MA: Cambridge, MA: Harvard University Press; London: William Heinemann Ltd., 1925).

God being a judge of all humankind.[13] It is posited that he may have learned of Moses when he visited Egypt, which still had a thriving Jewish community in his day. Could Plato have learned of this notion of the allotment of land to the gods from Moses as well?

We see that this spiritual allotment of nations under the authority of pagan gods was a worldview shared amongst many ancient peoples. Earthly regions and authorities had heavenly authorities over them. The question then becomes, how did ancient cultures share such a view? Did everyone borrow the belief from previous civilizations or did they all possess a sliver of truth from past history that was reinterpreted within each religious worldview? It's actually a bit of both, but regarding the Greeks, the likelihood is that ancient Greece borrowed from the ancient Near East.

As Westerners, we often learn that so much of our language and culture has its origins in Greco-Roman culture. What may surprise some is how much of the Greek worldview had its origins in the ancient Near East, which includes the Bible's Hebrew worldview. And that worldview includes religion.

Be aware that Greek mythology is not monolithic. Different traditions relate different versions of their myths, from Homeric and Orphic to Hesiodic and others. Rather than getting bogged down in the academia of the variations, I will try to stick with those most relevant to the storyline of the *Judah Maccabee* novels.

Readers of the Chronicles series of novels are familiar with the theology of cosmic mountains as residences of deity and connection points between heaven and earth. The council of El and Ba'al's Mount Zaphon (Sapan), the Watchers on Mount Hermon, Yahweh and his divine council on Mount Sinai and later Mount Zion are all carried over by Greek religion into the assembly of gods under Zeus on Mount Olympus.

---

[13] Peter J. Leithart, "Did Plato Read Moses?: Middle Grace and Moral Consensus," *Biblical Horizons Occasional Paper No. 23* (Niceville, FL: Biblical Horizons, 1995).

Zeus himself had become a storm god called the "Cloud Gatherer,"[14] just like Ba'al the storm god was called the "Cloud-rider" before him,[15] and Yahweh as the true storm God "rode a swift cloud" of historical judgment.[16]

Rephaim

Readers of the Chronicles are familiar with the biblical creatures called *Rephaim.* As I have explained elsewhere, this name, used synonymously at times with *Anakim* in the Old Testament. It was given to the giants in the land of Canaan defined as mighty giant warriors that Yahweh dedicated to destruction.[17] This is because the Rephaim/Anakim were considered to have come from the ancient Nephilim before the Flood, who were described as "mighty warriors of old, men of renown, (Genesis 6:4), whose rebellion was partly responsible for the Flood of God's judgment.

But there is more. The Ugaritic word for *Rephaim* has its roots in the Canaanite myths of mighty dead warrior kings who ruled from the underworld. They did so as a council and were called upon to legitimize earthly kings above. So, when Isaiah addressed the king of Babylon in Isaiah 14, he mocked the king's pursuit of greatness by likening him to the Rephaim in Sheol (underworld). Unlike the deluded pagan mythology, Rephaim were not mighty lords in the underworld. They were actually shades of their previous existence, with no power at all in Sheol. Isaiah wrote that the Babylonian king would ultimately die and

---

[14] Homer, *Illiad* 1.511. "The Gatherer of Clouds" was a common epithet Homer used. F. Graf, "Zeus," in *Dictionary of Deities and Demons in the Bible*, ed. Karel van der Toorn, Bob Becking, and Pieter W. van der Horst (Leiden; Boston; Köln; Grand Rapids, MI; Cambridge: Brill; Eerdmans, 1999), 934.

[15] N. Wyatt, *Religious Texts from Ugarit*, 2nd ed., *The Biblical Seminar*, vol. 53 (London: Sheffield Academic Press, 2002). Charioteer [Rider] of the Clouds also appears in these texts: KTU 1.2:4.8-9; 1.3:4:4, 6, 26; 1.4:3:10, 18; 1.4:5:7, 60; 1.10:1:7; 1.10:3:21, 36; 1.19:1:43; 1.92:37, 39.

[16] 1 Samuel 22:7-12; Psalm 104:3-4; Isaiah 19:1; and others.

[17] Deuteronomy 2:10-11, 20; 3:11, 13; Joshua 12:4; 13:12; 1 Chronicles 20:4-8; 2 Samuel 21:16-22; Joshua 11:21-23. Rephaim were also connected to the Anakim, as were the Zamzummim, the Emim, Amorites, and others. See Brian Godawa, *When Giants Were Upon the Earth: The Watchers, the Nephilim, and the Biblical Cosmic War of the Seed*, (Allen, TX: Warrior Poet Publishing, 2014), 70-74; 141-143. Brian Godawa, *When Watchers Ruled the Nations: Pagan Gods at War with Israel's God and the Spiritual World of the Bible* (Allen, TX: Warrior Poet Publishing, 2020, 2021), 143-144, 318-322.

be just as weak and powerless in death as the Rephaim actually were. Isaiah was defying this Canaanite divine glorification of an underworld council of Rephaim warrior kings (see also Isaiah 26:14):

> Isaiah 14:9–11
> Sheol beneath is stirred up to meet you [king of Babylon] when you come; it rouses the [Rephaim] to greet you, all who were leaders of the earth; it raises from their thrones all who were kings of the nations. All of them will answer and say to you: 'You too have become as weak as we! You have become like us!' Your pomp is brought down to Sheol, the sound of your harps; maggots are laid as a bed beneath you, and worms are your covers.

And there is yet more. The New Testament provides the likely origin of the Ugaritic deification of Rephaim in the underworld. In Jude and 2 Peter, we learn that the divine angelic beings whose rebellion against Yahweh created the monstrous Nephilim were punished by imprisonment in Tartarus, the Greek name for the deepest part of Hades (or Sheol).[18]

The Greek mythographer Apollodorus described Tartarus as "a place of infernal darkness as distant from the earth as the earth from the sky."[19]And there is no Hebrew equivalent of Tartarus, which means the Apostles were expressing ideas common with Greek religion.

> 2 Peter 2:4–5
> For if God did not spare angels when they sinned, but cast them into [Tartarus] and committed them to chains of gloomy darkness to be kept until the judgment; if he did not spare the ancient world, but preserved Noah…

---

[18] In the Intertestamental period, "Sons of God" was unfortunately simplified in Greek to "angels," which obscures the full meaning. Thus, the New Testament authors pick up that looser terminology for their audience. The angels of Jude 6 and 2 Peter 2:4 are the Sons of God of Genesis 6:1. For more details of this event, see the book that was used as a source for Jude and Peter: 1 Enoch 12:4, 10:12; 63:10.

[19] Apollodorus, Trans., Robin Hard, *The Library of Greek Mythology* (Oxford: Oxford University Press, 1997), 1.1.2, p 27.

> Jude 6
> And the angels who did not stay within their own position of authority, but left their proper dwelling, he has kept in eternal chains under gloomy darkness until the judgment of the great day.

English translations commonly translate the Greek word *tartarosas* in 2 Peter 2 as *hell.* But it is not hell. It is Tartarus. *The New International Dictionary of New Testament Theology and Exegesis* explains that in Greek mythology Tartarus "denoted a deep abyss, far beneath Hades...Various myths revolved around it; many Titans were said to have been cast into Tartarus by Zeus...which reflects the Jewish apocalyptic view of Tartarus as the place where the disobedient angels were sent after they rebelled against the Lord. This place, however, is not identified as the actual place of punishment for these angels. Rather, they are being 'held' there temporarily as prisoners until judgment is meted out on them."[20]

So did the Hebrews draw from the Greeks or did the Greeks draw from the Hebrews? Language and cultural analysis like that of Assyriologist Amar Annus has shown that the Greek mythology of the Titans is linguistically derived from the Rephaim of the Semitic Middle East.[21] And its storyline bears an influence from the ancient Near Eastern Rephaim narrative as well.

In Greek religion, the Titans were the first generation of twelve gods birthed by the sky god Ouranos and earth goddess Gaia. One of those Titans, Kronos, overthrew Ouranos to be king of the gods. He then sought to keep his own children from doing the same to him. Those children were Zeus and the Olympian gods.

---

[20] Moisés Silva, ed., *New International Dictionary of New Testament Theology and Exegesis* (Grand Rapids, MI: Zondervan, 2014), 458-459.

[21] Amar Annus, "Are There Greek Rephaim? On the Etymology of Greek Meropes and Titanes," *Ugarit Forschungen*, 1999, Vol 31, 13–30.

GODS OF OLYMPUS	
Children of Kronos	**Children of Zeus**
Zeus: king of the gods, sky	**Hephaestus**: god of fire, forging, volcanoes
Poseidon: god of sea and elements	**Ares**: god of war, violence, bloodshed
Pluto: god of underworld (not Olympian)	**Athena**: goddess of wisdom, war
Hera: goddess of marriage and childbirth	**Apollo**: god of sun, prophecy, archery, plague
Demeter: goddess of harvest, agriculture	**Artemis**: goddess of the hunt, virginity
Hestia: goddess of the hearth, domesticity	**Aphrodite**: goddess of love, passion
	Hermes: messenger of the gods, travel
	Dionysus: god of wine, festivity, ecstasy

TABLE OF OLYMPIAN GODS. There were only 12 Olympians, but there are 14 in this chart. Pluto was not considered Olympian because he resided and ruled in the underworld. The other Olympians are children of Zeus. Dionysus or Hestia were omitted depending on the source tradition[22].

But Kronos was ultimately unsuccessful in his coup as Zeus and his siblings subsequently overthrew Kronos and the other Titans in a ten-year battle called the Titanomachy. This resulted in a succession of the new gods over the former gods. Zeus then divided the cosmos, or "heavens and earth," through allotment between himself as ruler of the sky, Poseidon as ruler of the sea, and Pluto as ruler of the underworld. All the gods held the earth in common.[23] Though this allotment was a kind of equality with some freedom on the part of the gods, Zeus nevertheless as eldest remained king of the gods on Olympus. He often intervened with his superior will.

Back to our story. The victorious Olympians imprisoned the Titans in Tartarus, so Greek mythographer Hesiod called the Titans the "earth-born," which referred to being beneath the earth in the underworld, and therefore chthonic deities. The residue of biblical truth about divine Rephaim in the underworld seeps through the twisted distortions of pagan storytelling.

---

[22] William F. Hansen, *Classical Mythology: A Guide to the Mythical World of the Greeks and Romans* (Oxford: Oxford University Press, 2005), 250.

[23]Apollodorus, *Library of Greek Mythology* 1.2. In Homer, *Iliad*, 15:185-195, they draw lots to receive their territories.

This Greek Titanomachy that resulted in the overthrow of the high god Kronos by Zeus and the Olympians has its origins in the biblical rebellion that has been a foundational story for all three of my Chronicles series of novels: the Sons of God in Genesis 6:1-4.

As described above, 2 Peter 2:4-5 calls it the sin of the angels in Noah's day, who were cast into Tartarus as punishment, and who Jude 6-7 explains as leaving their own "proper dwelling" in heaven to go after "strange flesh" by mating with human women, resulting in their "being kept in eternal chains of gloomy darkness until their judgment."

Though there is no naming of a lead "god" in the biblical text, there is one named in the book of 1 Enoch, which Jude quoted and paraphrased: Shemihazah (alternate spellings: Semyaza, Semjaza), who led 200 Sons of God, called Watchers, in the Genesis 6 rebellion. 1 Enoch 6 tells us that Shemihazah called the other Watchers up to Mount Hermon to take an oath together against the Creator, whereupon they spread out and taught humans forbidden knowledge of sorceries, sexualities, war, and occult magic (1 Enoch 7-8).

Just like the divinely pretentious usurper Helel ben Shachar of Isaiah 14, and like the Titans of Greek mythology, Shemihazah and his fallen angelic army are judged by being cast down and imprisoned in the underworld below the earth—more precisely, in Tartarus:

> 1 Enoch 14:5
> From now on you will not be able to ascend into heaven unto all eternity, but you shall remain inside the earth, imprisoned all the days of eternity.
>
> 2 Peter 2:4
> For if God did not spare angels when they sinned, but cast them into [Tartarus] and committed them to chains of gloomy darkness to be kept until the judgment…

As explained above, this Watcher rebellion of Genesis 6 and 1 Enoch is most likely the origin of the Greek myth of the Titanomachy. It repeats the pattern of God's judgment upon the divinely pretentious who would violate Yahweh's order, would attempt an ascension of heavenly power, but be brought down to the underworld in judgment. But the Greek myth subverts the Hebrew narrative by making Zeus and the Olympians successful in their rebellion against the Titans. It's the most common kind of alteration across all counter-narratives in history: the villains are made heroes and the heroes made villains.

There is another war in Greek mythology often confused with the Titanomachy. It is called the Gigantomachy, and it is a later war of giants on earth against the Olympian gods. Though there is no one-to-one correspondence, the Titans are more in line with the Rephaim of ancient Canaan that the Bible links with the earthly giants. But the giants of the Greek Gigantomachy are more akin to the Nephilim giants of Genesis 6 and their consequent hostility against the Watchers as the book of 1 Enoch describes. I tell a biblically-oriented version of both the Gigantomachy and the Titanomachy between the Nephilim giants and their Watcher gods in my novel *Enoch Primordial.*

The Genesis Sons of God/Nephilim narrative continues with the Rephaim and Anakim in the Promised Land of Canaan (Numbers 13:32-33), and that influence can also be found in the later Greek narrative of the golden "Heroic Age" of mighty warriors that resulted from the sexual union of the Olympian gods with humans. In contrast with the evil nature of the Bible's human/god hybrids, many Greek human/god hybrids were good guys, like Perseus, Heracles, and Bellerophon, who would found cities and engage in deeds of valor. It was considered a more mythological age that ended with the Trojan War. But it was yet another example of pagan mythology distorting the ancient Near Eastern historical narrative as expressed more truthfully in the Hebrew Scriptures.

Sidebar
The Storm God's Overthrow of the Sky God

The succession of gods through the overthrowing of a sky god by a lower storm god is another component of ancient Near Eastern religion that the Greeks borrowed and repurposed. In Hurrian and Hittite mythology, Kumarbi, the "father of the gods," emasculated his father Anu, the god of heaven (reflected in the Greek god Kronos emasculating his father, Ouranos, the god of heaven). In turn, then the Hurrian storm god Teshub overthrew Kumarbi to be enthroned as king of the gods in Mitanni. So then the storm god Zeus overthrew Kronos to become king of the gods in Greece.[24]

In some theological interpretations of Ezekiel 28 and Isaiah 14, the prophecies against the kings of Tyre and Babylon are interpreted as spiritual analogies for the fall of the *satan* (referred to as "Helel ben Shachar" in Isaiah 14). In this interpretation, it is possible that the succession of the storm god overthrowing the sky god of heaven in pagan mythology represents the *satan*'s original attempt to overthrow Yahweh and seek enthronement. The difference, of course, would be that in the biblical version of the story, the lesser god failed and was thrown down to the underworld.

> Isaiah 14:13–15
> 'You [Helel ben Shachar] said in your heart, 'I will ascend to heaven; above the stars [divine beings] of God I will set my throne on high; I will sit on the mount of assembly in the far reaches of the north; I will ascend above the heights of the clouds; I will make myself like the Most High.' But you are brought down to Sheol, to the far reaches of the pit."

In this interpretive context, heathen Gentile nations prefer to change the failure of the *satan*'s attempted insurrection into their storm god's successful coup to justify their rejection of the Most High. Of course, it must be conceded that the biblical story was not the first written account

[24] Hans Gustav Guterbock, "The Hittite Version of the Hurrian Kumarbi Myths: Oriental Forerunners of Hesiod," *American Journal of Archaeology*, Vol. 52, No. 1 (Jan. - Mar., 1948), pp. 123-134.

of these events. It was, however, the truest version God revealed through his prophets. If the first witness to write a narrative of events is corrupt or prejudicial, it matters not how early his account is.

Leviathan and Hydra

Leviathan is a supernatural monster that shows up in every Chronicles novel to date. That is because it is the Bible's sea dragon of chaos that symbolizes chaos's ongoing struggle against God's orderly kingdom and its growth. I have written an entire booklet about this most interesting creature explaining its biblical origins and development.[25]

For the sake of explaining its place in the *Judah Maccabee* novels and its Greek mythology counterpart, I will draw attention to one of Scripture's many passages about Leviathan, Psalm 74.

Here, we have a poetic passage describing the Red Sea crossing of the Exodus in terms of Yahweh's spiritual victory over Pharaoh and the forces of chaos. God's liberation of Israel from the chaos of Egypt, which led to his subsequent establishment of covenantal order at Sinai, is described as Yahweh having power over the sea and the sea dragon of chaos, Leviathan:

> Psalm 74:13–17
> You [Yahweh] divided the sea [Red Sea] by your might;
> you broke the heads of the sea monsters on the waters.
> You crushed the heads of Leviathan;
> you gave him as food for the creatures of the wilderness.
> Yours is the day, yours also the night;
> you have established the heavenly lights and the sun.
> You have fixed all the boundaries of the earth;
> you have made summer and winter.

---

[25] Brian Godawa, Leviathan and Behemoth: Giant Chaos Monsters in the Bible (Allen, TX: Warrior Poet Publishing, 2022).

As I have noted before, the description of Leviathan here includes it having numerous heads. How many heads, it does not say. But the Canaanite equivalent of Leviathan had seven, and in the book of Revelation (ch. 13), the sea dragon symbolizing the chaos enemy of God also has seven heads.

The key to its symbolism lies in the description of God giving the defeated Leviathan as food for the creatures of the wilderness, a common motif in the Bible that symbolizes military victory over one's enemies.[26] Yahweh fought for Israel against Pharaoh and his forces of chaos and won the victory over them. Perhaps it is Pharaoh himself who is symbolized in Leviathan, a similar comparison made in Ezekiel 29:1-5. There Pharaoh Hophra is mocked as "the great dragon that lies in the streams," who would be "cast out into the wilderness" as food for the birds and beasts.

Despite God establishing his covenant order and his people through his redemptive acts, God never fully destroys chaos and sin in the current heavens and earth. Notice in this passage by Isaiah that Leviathan, who was supposedly crushed and eaten up in the wilderness of the Exodus in Psalm 74, is still around until God defeats Leviathan, the ultimate symbol of chaos, for the last time in the eschaton. Leviathan is a symbol of a spiritual truth:

> Isaiah 27:1
> In that day the LORD with his hard and great and strong sword will punish Leviathan the fleeing serpent, Leviathan the twisting serpent, and he will slay the dragon that is in the sea.

There are strong ties between Leviathan and the sea dragons of chaos in the myths of Israel's neighbors, including Canaan/Phoenicia, Hurrian/Hittite, Babylon/Mesopotamia, Egypt, and Greece. Though there is not a one-to-one correspondence in Greek mythology with

---

26 Jeremiah 12:9; Ezekiel 32:4; 39:17-19; Revelation 19:17-18. For Second Temple examples of the feast of Leviathan and Behemoth, see 4 Ezra 6:47-52; 2 Apoc. Bar. 29:4; and 1 Enoch 60: 7-9, 24.

Leviathan, there are a few monsters who show at least a common source of serpentine hostility to the forces of good.

Typhon was one of the early gods that Gaia and Tartarus birthed in revenge against the Giants the Olympians conquered in the Gigantomachy of primeval days. Typhon was usually conceived as a humanoid figure from the waist up, with serpent tails for legs, and who also had multiple heads. But one of his progenies closely resembled the Levant's Leviathan: the Hydra of Lernea.

Lernea was a special area of springs and a marshy lake near the east coast of southern Greece's Peloponnesian region. The lake was considered an entrance to the underworld of Hades, and the Hydra was a chthonic guardian of that portal. The Hydra was described as an enormous sea serpent with multiple heads, six or nine or fifty, depending on the tradition, and one of those heads was immortal. Its breath and blood were poisonous.

King Eurystheus commissioned Heracles to kill the Hydra for his Second Labor of monster killing. Heracles used fiery arrows to draw the Hydra out into the open to battle with sword, club, and sickle. But when the Greek hero chopped off one of the serpentine heads, another two would grow in its place. So, Heracles conspired with his nephew Iolaus to kill the beast by using burning brands to cauterize the wound each time Heracles would cut off a head, thus inhibiting Hydra's ability to regenerate heads. Eventually, he cut off Hydra's immortal head and buried it. Then Heracles dipped his arrows in the blood of the dead Hydra to use as poisonous weapons in future exploits.[27]

So, Hydra was a sea dragon that brought chaos, much like Leviathan. And it was a guardian of the waters that led to Hades in Greek cosmology, much like Leviathan swam the waters of the Abyss that led to Sheol in Hebrew cosmology.

---

27 Apollodorus, Trans., Robin Hard, *The Library of Greek Mythology* (Oxford: Oxford University Press, 1997), 2.5.2, p. 74.

Zeus

Though there are many different versions of Greek mythology, the poet Hesiod (ca. 700 BC) and his book *Theogony* is one of the foremost references for the origins, identities, and stories of the Greek gods.[28] In it, we see a succession narrative of early gods overthrown by later gods.

As outlined earlier, First, there was Chaos and Gaia (earth) with Night and Day. Ouranos (sky) and Gaia (earth) birthed the first set of primordial gods called the Titans. One of those Titans, Kronos, ambushed his father Ouranos, castrated him, and separated him (sky) from Gaia (earth), their version of the separation of heaven and earth, a common component in most creation stories.[29]

Kronos then took over and mated with his sister goddess Rhea and they gave birth to three female deities—Hestia, Demeter, Hera—and three male deities—Pluto, Poseidon, and Zeus. But because Kronos did not want to be overthrown by his offspring as he had done to his father, he swallowed his children.

Rhea however tricked Kronos and got him to swallow a stone wrapped in swaddling clothes instead of the real Zeus. Zeus grew up and managed to get Kronos to vomit Zeus' siblings into the world. Along with those freed captives were several Cyclopes, one-eyed monsters who then provided the powerful weapon of thunderbolts to Zeus, a magical helmet of invisibility to Pluto, and a mighty trident to Poseidon.[30] The mountain Olympus became their home.

Zeus and the twelve Olympians defeated Kronos and the other Titans in the Titanomachy and imprisoned them in Tartarus, after which Zeus took his place as king of the gods and was allotted the sky as his

---

[28] Other main sources of Greek mythology scholars use, such as Homer, Orpheus, Apollodorus, Pausanius, and Greek historians such as Herodotus, Diodorus Siculus, and Plutarch, vary in some of their details.

[29] Hesiod, trans., Barry B. Powell, *The Poems of Hesiod: Theogony, Works and Days and the Shield of Herakles* (Oakland, CA: University of California Press, 2017), *Theogony* 95-145, pp. 36-41.

[30] Apollodorus, *Library of Greek Mythology* 1.1.5-2.1 pp. 27-28.

domain. He became known as a storm god with the epithet "Cloud-Gatherer."[31]

Though most people know about him having taken his sister goddess Hera as his wife, they may not be aware that Hera was his seventh and last wife. And Zeus was not even satisfied with only seven wives. A randy promiscuous adulterer, he also took many mistresses, both divine and human. He became known for fathering many gods, such as Apollo the sun god, Ares the god of war, and Athena goddess of war. But he also mated with mortal women to birth human/god hybrids, the most famous of which was Heracles.

There is little doubt that Zeus's sexual interaction with humans was modeled on the ancient Near Eastern narrative of the divine Sons of God mating with human daughters of men. Though Heracles was not a giant like the human/angel hybrid Nephilim, he was certainly in the category of the Hebrew *gibborim*, the mighty men of old, the men of renown (Genesis 6:4). His character reflected the excess of a demigod as well. He had extraordinary strength and extraordinary passions, including many sexual conquests of both men and women.

Like father, like son.

Zeus and the Abomination of Desolation

When Antiochus Epiphanes set up the "abomination of desolation" in the Jerusalem temple, he renamed it the temple of Zeus Olympian (2 Maccabees 6:2). But what did the abomination look like and what rituals did the king demand from the Jews? To answer that, we begin with the text of the Maccabees. 1 Maccabees is the least detailed. It simply states:

> 1 Maccabees 1:54-55 (LES)
> Now [the Seleucid officials] built an **abomination of desolation** on the [Jerusalem] altar, and in the cities around

[31] Homer, *Illiad* 1.511.

> Judah, they built altars. And at the windows of their houses and in the streets, they burned incense.
>
> 1 Maccabees 1: 44-47 (LES)
> And the king [Antiochus] sent letters by messengers to Jerusalem and the towns of Judah; he directed them … to build altars and sacred precincts and shrines for idols, to sacrifice swine and other unclean animals.

Ancient Jewish historian Josephus wrote, "And when the king had built an idol altar upon God's Altar, he slew swine upon it, and so offered a sacrifice."[32]

The word *abomination* in Hebrew (*siqqus*) was a word used in the context of physical images of pagan gods (idols) that Yahweh considered detestable in his presence.[33] The Hebrew word for *desolate* (*mesomem*) reinforced that alienation. It meant to make uninhabitable, thus implying the withdrawing of God's presence due to the presence of the abominable idol. Yahweh simply did not tolerate the worship of any gods before him (Exodus 20:3).

So the Hebrew conception in the phrase "abomination of desolation" involved the image of a false god's presence. Desolation did not require the temple's actual destruction, but simply the resultant withdrawal of God's presence due to the images/idols' religious pollution.

Josephus wrote that "the king [Antiochus Epiphanes] built an idol altar upon God's altar,"[34] which echoes 1 Maccabees 1:59: "…they were sacrificing on the altar [to Zeus] that was on [Yahweh's] altar for burnt sacrifices." We are told nowhere what the idol altar that was built upon Yahweh's altar may have looked like. Most assume the simple description of new stones placed upon the existing stones of the

---

[32] Josephus, Antiquities 12.4 (253) Flavius Josephus and William Whiston, *The Works of Josephus: Complete and Unabridged* (Peabody: Hendrickson, 1987), 324.

[33] Deuteronomy 29:17; 2 Kings 23:24; 2 Chronicles 15:8; Jeremiah 13:27, 16:8, 32:34; Ezekiel 20:7, 32:23.

[34] Josephus, *Antiquities* 12.5.4 [12.253].

Jerusalem altar. But why would there be a need to add additional stones to an existing functioning altar? Perhaps they were adding something distinctly Greek to that altar.

The implication is that the stones may have been actual idol images of some kind as those indicated by the Hebrew terms defined above, *siqqus mesomem* ("pagan idol that pollutes") and causes Yahweh to leave. Though we know Antiochus Epiphanes renamed the Jerusalem temple for Zeus Olympian, we also know that altars to Zeus could include his image as well as those of other deities, such as Athena.[35]

A common ancient view of the abomination of desolation was that of Roman philosopher Porphyry (AD 234-305), who suggested that it was an actual statue of Zeus enthroned on the altar.[36] Such large statues of Zeus were known in other Greek-conquered cities. Ancient historians wrote of a golden Zeus statue 12 cubits (18 feet) high in the precinct of the Babylonian temple, a 40-foot-tall golden Zeus statue at the temple of Belus, and a 72-foot-tall bronze Zeus statue at Tarantum.[37]

While some recent interpretations reject the possibility of a statue on the altar, it would make sense to place such a statue of Zeus into the Holy of Holies because that inner sanctuary was supposed to be God's throne and the Ark of the Covenant his footstool. Such an act would represent Zeus taking over Yahweh's throne. But the Holy of Holies is not the altar of burnt sacrifice. How would an idol change that structure?

The Anchor Bible Commentary suggests the "abomination of desolation" may have consisted of three meteorite cult-stones (*massebot*), which represented the God of the Jews (Yahweh/Zeus); his female divine consort, the Queen of Heaven (Anat/Athena); and his divine son, Dionysus.[38] Though entirely speculative, this would

---

[35] This is the case with the famous altar of Zeus at Pergamum that includes Athena.

[36] John Collins and Peter W. Flint, Ed., *The Book of Daniel: Composition and Reception Volume 2* (Boston: Brill, 2001), 677.

[37] James Alan Montgomery, *A Critical and Exegetical Commentary on the Book of Daniel* (Edinburgh: T&T Clark, 1959), 193-194.

[38] Jonathan A. Goldstein, *I Maccabees: A New Translation with Introduction and Commentary, vol. 41*, Anchor Yale Bible (New Haven; London: Yale University Press, 2008), 224.

synchronize well with the idol worship of cult standing stones (*massebot*) that Jews had a long history of engaging in. Solomon had constructed *massebot* for Ba'al, Molech, and Astarte (2 Kings 23:13-14) and King Ahab set one up for Ba'al in Samaria (2 Kings 3:2; 10:27). At various times in Judah's and Israel's history, they would raise standing stones and other pagan cult objects "on every high hill and under every green tree" (1 Kings 14:23; 2 Kings 17:10).

Though the Jews would not have required cult-stones to be meteorites,[39] the Greek king would find commonality with *massebot* in the famous temple of Apollo at Delphi which housed the Omphalos, a large conical meteorite stone believed to have been placed at that location by Zeus to mark it as the "navel" or center of the earth.[40]

As we have suspected the high priest Menelaus to have counseled Antiochus in this matter, he might have likely suggested a subversive way of syncretizing the gods of Canaan with the gods of Greece. Zeus had already been worshipped in Syrian cities as Ba'al-Shamem and his consort was Anat (Athena). So *massebot* representing gods interchangeable between Canaan and Greece might be one way of seeking the smoothest transition.

But a strong argument against this *massebot* view is that Antiochus was extremely hostile to the Jewish religion and sought to deny them their Torah distinctives, so it would not be as likely he would seek a syncretist blending as opposed to an explicit and hostile replacement of deities.[41]

Though an attempt to decode this nefarious abomination of desolation leaves us with a plethora of questions and unproven

---

[39] "Standing Stones," Brian Godawa, *The Spiritual World of Jezebel and Elijah* (Allen, TX: Warrior Poet Publishing, 2021), 97-99.

[40] Robin Hard, *The Routledge Handbook of Greek Mythology, 8th edition* (Oxon, OX: Routledge, 1928, 2020), 136-137.

[41] Bible scholar Johan Lust concludes, "These passages seem to identify the 'abomination of desolation' with an 'idol altar,' a kind of superstructure built upon the altar of the Lord. No mention is made of a statue of a pagan deity, nor of meteorites." Johan Lust, "Cult Sacrifice in Daniel. The Tamil and the Abomination of Desolation," John J. Collins and Peter W. Flint, Eds., *The Book of Daniel: Composition and Reception Volume 2* (Boston: Brill, 2001), 684.

possibilities, it remains a fascinating subject for fictional speculation in the *Judah Maccabee* novels.

One side note about abominable images in the temple. In the *Judah Maccabee* novels, the corrupt, idolatrous high priest Menelaus is depicted as installing an olivewood statue of cherubim in the Holy of Holies to replace the cherubim Solomon created (1 Kings 6:23-28) but had been missing since the Babylonian exile. Whereas Solomon's standing cherubim had spread wings tip-to-tip over the Ark of the Covenant, Menelaus's replacement was a statue of cherubim entwined in sexual union. This outrageous image is rooted in the incipient Jewish mysticism of the day that became Merkavah, a forerunner of Kabbalah mysticism. Their interest in ascents into heaven and visions of Yahweh's heavenly throne chariot was drawn from Ezekiel's visions and is reflected in the books of Enoch from that time period onward. Some strains of such mysticism described spiritual union with God in sexual terms.

This shocking fictional embellishment is rooted in a Talmudic tradition and other Midrashim that argued that, at one time, the cherubim in the most holy place were indeed sculpted in this bizarre sexual position.[42] One scholar even connects the incident to the time of Antiochus Epiphanes's reign.[43] Sometimes, truth is stranger than fiction.

My novels also have Menelaus offer 300 silver drachmas as a sacrifice to Zeus in Antioch. This was actually an act that the previous high priest Jason performed in a sacrifice to Heracles in Tyre (2 Maccabees 4:18-20). But since Menelaus had performed "many acts of sacrilege" according to the Maccabean author (4:39), it was certainly

---

[42] Rabbi Qetina and Rabbi Shimeon ben Laqish from the 3rd century, Rashi in the 11th, and other Midrashim.

[43] Raphael Patai, *The Hebrew Goddess Third Enlarged Edition* (Detroit: Wayne State University Press, 1967,1978, 1990), 84-85.

not out of character for Menelaus and maintained the spirit of what had been going on by both Hellenizing high priests.

Regarding the idolatrous activities Antiochus imposed, 2 Maccabees describes in more detail the imposition of Greek gods upon the Jews (bold emphasis added):

> 2 Maccabees 6:1-6 (RSV)
> Not long after this, the king sent an Athenian senator to compel the Jews to forsake the laws of their ancestors and no longer to live by the laws of God; **also to pollute the temple in Jerusalem and to call it the temple of Olympian Zeus, and to call the one in Gerizim the temple of Zeus-the-Friend-of-Strangers, as did the people who lived in that place**.
>
> Harsh and utterly grievous was the onslaught of evil. For the temple was filled with debauchery and reveling by the **Gentiles, who dallied with prostitutes and had intercourse with women within the sacred precincts**, and besides brought in things for sacrifice that were unfit. The altar was **covered with abominable offerings that were forbidden by the laws**. People could neither keep the sabbath, nor observe the festivals of their ancestors, nor so much as confess themselves to be Jews.

After this, the writer of 2 Maccabees, adds that, at a festival for Dionysus, the Greek god of bacchanalia, the Jews were also forced to wear "wreaths of ivy and to walk in the procession in honor of Dionysus" (6:7). What the writer is too diplomatic in describing is that the festival's procession, called the Dionysia, involved pulling a cart featuring large wooden or bronze *phalloi*, images of phalluses on poles.

This is because the celebration's origin was rooted in a mythical incident in which the city of Athens rejected a gifted statue of Dionysus, so the god sent a plague on the male citizens' genitals. Only accepting the cult of Dionysus healed their epidemic malady.[44]

But back to Zeus.

According to 2 Maccabees, the pagan worship of Zeus involved temple prostitutes in the temple mount's sacred precincts. But again, this behavior was already well-known in Israel's history of Canaanite idol worship, so it would be another familiar addition to the imposed apostasy.

But the focus of worship was an idol altar built upon the Jerusalem altar of burnt offerings upon which unclean animals such as pigs were sacrificed. This idolatrous altar was considered the "abomination of desolation" predicted by the prophet Daniel:

> Daniel 11:31
> Forces from him [Antiochus Epiphanes] shall appear and profane the temple and fortress [in Jerusalem], and shall take away the regular burnt offering. And they shall set up the **abomination that makes desolate**.

This same abomination of desolation is implicated in another prophecy of Daniel that foretells the Maccabean incidents. And this one brings in the spiritual powers involved in the incident.

> Daniel 8:9–13
> Out of one of them came a little horn [Antiochus Epiphanes], which grew exceedingly great toward the south, toward the east, and toward the glorious land. It grew great, even to the host of heaven. And some of the host and some of the stars it threw down to the ground and trampled on them. It became great, even as great as the

---

[44] "Dionysia," Wikipedia: https://en.wikipedia.org/wiki/Dionysia

"The date of the desecration of the temple in the month just before the winter solstice (Kislev) may have coincided with a festival of Dionysus. Antiochus IV's Athenian expert may have suggested imposing on the Jews the 'rustic Dionysia,' which in Athens were celebrated in the month of Posideon=Kislev; indeed, the author at I 1:54–55 stresses that the rites were observed in the country towns." Jonathan A. Goldstein, *I Maccabees: A New Translation with Introduction and Commentary*, vol. 41, Anchor Yale Bible (New Haven; London: Yale University Press, 2008), 155.

> Prince of the host. And the regular burnt offering was taken away from him, and the place of his sanctuary was overthrown. And a host will be given over to it together with the regular burnt offering because of transgression, and it will throw truth to the ground, and it will act and prosper. Then I heard a holy one speaking, and another holy one said to the one who spoke, "For how long is the vision concerning the regular burnt offering, the **transgression that makes desolate**, and the giving over of the sanctuary and host to be trampled underfoot?"

As explained earlier, this little horn is a descendant of the great single horn of the goat that represented Alexander the Great of Macedon. After the Greek conqueror's death, four of his generals divided his kingdom. Out of one of those generals, Seleucus, came this little horn, Antiochus IV Epiphanes.

Those who would seek to find a merely earthly historical narrative here see Antiochus growing great and, specifically regarding the "glorious land" of Israel, he would overcome the "Prince of the host," interpreted as the Jewish high priest, from whom the regular burnt offering would be taken. A host of Jews would then be "given over" in both war and slavery to Antiochus, who then tramples the temple and God's people underfoot. But this earthly naturalistic interpretation does not take into account the supernatural context that includes the spiritual powers at war in the heavenlies.

First, the context of this prophecy within the book of Daniel is quite supernatural. The chapter before it, Daniel 7, charted out the four Gentile kingdoms ending in Rome that results in the ascension of the Son of Man (Jesus) to his throne in heaven. We read of "ten thousand times ten thousand" who stood before that fiery throne and "the court sat in judgment" (Daniel 7:10). This phrase is always used of Yahweh's heavenly host of divine beings that surrounds him, often in judgment.[45]

---

[45] Jude 14:15; Psalm 68:17; Revelation 5:11; Deuteronomy 33:2-3 LXX.

So, when Daniel 8:10-11 refers to the little horn Antiochus Epiphanes, becoming "as great as the Prince of the host," this is not a mere reference to a human high priest. It is likely a supernatural reference to Antiochus Epiphanes's godlike pretensions ("god manifest") in takeover of Yahweh's house (the temple of his presence), and with it, spiritual authority over Israel.

In Daniel, the Aramaic word for "prince" (*sar*) is used of spiritual princes over nations (Daniel 10:13, 20-21). Daniel interprets for us later in the passage that Antiochus "becoming as great as the Prince of the host" was another way of saying that the little horn "shall rise up against the Prince of princes," that "in his own mind he shall become great" (8:25). In truth, he would not be a god, "and he shall be broken—but not by human hands" (8:25). This was spiritual warfare with historic consequences. There is only one Prince of princes in both heaven and earth: Yahweh.[46] And there is only one Prince of the host: Yahweh, God of hosts.[47] And this Prince of the host of heaven is the Angel of Yahweh (Joshua 5:14-15), who is ultimately the preincarnate Jesus (Revelation 9:11-16), our high priest (Hebrews 4:14).

Daniel defines this Prince's "host," including the stars, as the "host of heaven" (8:10). I have described elsewhere that "host of heaven" in the Bible is not merely a reference to the sun, moon, and stars, but also to angelic Sons of God (Job 38:7), other angels (Psalms 148:2-3), and gods of the nations (Deuteronomy 4:12-20).[48]

This leads to the most natural conclusion that this symbolic prophecy of stars "being thrown to the ground and trampled" is fulfilled in the overthrow of heavenly powers along with their earthly counterparts. This is the conflict of gods over nations we established earlier. When the pagan ruler Antiochus captured the temple and

---

[46] "Prince of the host" in Hebrew was the same phrase used of the Angel of Yahweh, Yahweh himself (Joshua 5:14).

[47] Psalm 59:5, 89:8; Isaiah 10:24, 33; Jeremiah 5:14, 15:16, 38:17; Amos 4:13, 5:27.

[48] See also Deuteronomy 32:8-9, 17, 43. For detailed investigation of stars as divine, see Brian Godawa *When Watchers Ruled the Nations: Pagan Gods at War with Israel's God and the Spiritual World of the Bible* (Allen, TX: Warrior Poet Publishing, 2021), 27-37.

profaned it, some of Yahweh's heavenly host were "given over to it together with the regular burnt offering because of the transgression" (Daniel 8:12). The heavenly conflict mirrored earthly conflict, and because Israel transgressed against Yahweh in her unfaithfulness, this empowered the pagan earthly and heavenly rulers to maintain temporary power over Yahweh's holy temple. On earth as it is in heaven (Matthew 6:10b).

When Daniel hears a "holy one" speaking to another "holy one," some think that "holy one" is a reference to Israelites or "saints," as it is sometimes translated. But "holy one" is tricky because it is used of both human Israelites[49] and heavenly divine beings around God's throne, as well as Yahweh himself.[50] So context would dictate the meaning. And Daniel's context contains both. But when it comes to Daniel's visions, he explicitly describes the holy ones as heavenly beings.

For example, in Daniel 4, the prophet sees a vision where he defines "a watcher, **a holy one**, came down from heaven" (4:13) and those Watchers make decrees, "decisions by the word of the **holy ones**" (4:17). And let us not forget that in Daniel 8, the original passage we are studying, Daniel is also having a vision of these holy ones who are "of heaven," not of earth.

So the context of Daniel 8 is clearly a story of the earthly Antiochus trampling god's temple and people underfoot, but with the simultaneous spiritual reality of the heavenly host over Israel being temporarily overcome.

The "transgression that makes desolate" is therefore a reference to the sin of Israel that brought on the abomination of desolation, the imposition of Zeus worship with its altars and pagan ritual behaviors coupled with the spiritual power that comes with such earthly victory.

---

[49] Daniel 7:18, 21-22, 25, 27; 8:24; Psalm 34:9; 16:3; 30:4.

[50] Psalm 89:5, 7; Deuteronomy 33:2; Zechariah 14:5; Jude 14; Job 15:15.

Yes, the pagan king Antiochus is responsible for setting up the idol, but unfortunately, many Jews embraced it and engaged in idol worship.

But of course, Yahweh's will is never ultimately thwarted, and it is Yahweh's hand that defeats both Antiochus's earthly power and that of the spiritual powers working behind the scenes (Daniel 8:24-25). As king Nebuchadnezzar would ultimately learn:

> Daniel 4:35
> [Yahweh] does according to his will among the host of
>   heaven
>   and among the inhabitants of the earth;
> and none can stay his hand
>   or say to him, "What have you done?"

Hera and Heracles

Hera, one of the original Titans' six children, was the goddess of marriage and childbirth, but not motherhood. She is described as noble and matronly in beauty, with the epithet of being "cow-eyed," an evident connection with the cattle of her patron city of Argos, the most ancient in Greece.[51] This urban connection is why some scholars have argued for her matriarchal rule as the (singular) Great Goddess of Greece's original religion. More explanation of this below in the section titled "Gaia."

As Zeus's seventh and final wife, Hera was both jealous and vengeful against her promiscuous philandering husband. So much so that she engaged in acts of sabotage on the lovers and offspring of Zeus's affairs. Hera sought to stop births of Zeus's bastard children and turned some of his mistresses into animals. She also defied Zeus's command for the gods to stay out of the Trojan War. Helen of Troy was the offspring of one of Zeus's affairs with Nemesis, a goddess of vengeance. At one point, Zeus became so angered with Hera's jealous

---

[51] Robin Hard, *The Routledge Handbook of Greek Mythology, 8th edition* (Oxon, OX: Routledge, 1928, 2020), 119-120.

acts that he strung her up with weights attached to her feet like a Greek slave would be punished.[52]

But the weight of Hera's jealousy was focused mostly on Heracles, the last offspring of Zeus's dalliances with mortals, and whose name ironically meant "glory of Hera."

The goddess sought to delay Heracles's birth. She sent two snakes to kill him as an infant, and then drove him mad as an adult, which resulted in Heracles murdering his own family. Most notably, Hera placed Heracles into the service of a Mycenaen king to engage in his famous Twelve Labors as penance for familicide and a means through which he could gain deification and immortality.[53]

During each of the labors, Hera sought to undermine the mighty warrior. Some of the labors are reproduced in the *Judah Maccabee* novels. Here are all twelve from the original myths:

1) **Kill the Nemean Lion**, whose skin was impenetrable to weapons. Raised by Hera to terrorize the hills of Nemea.
2) **Slay the many-headed Hydra** of Lerna, where Hercules drew some of its poisonous blood for his arrows. Hera raised this monster with the purpose of killing Heracles.
3) **Capture the Ceryneian Hind** sacred to Artemis, whose antlers were golden.
4) **Ensnare the Erymanthian Boar**, a huge wild monster and vessel of Artemis's wrath.
5) **Clean the Augean stables** of cattle filth in one day.
6) **Slaughter the Stymphalian birds**, man-eating avians with bronze beaks and sharp metal wings, which Ares created.
7) **Fetch the Cretan bull** Poseidon was sent as a sacrifice but which had been kept alive, eliciting Poseidon's rage at King Minos.

---

[52] Hard, *The Routledge Handbook,* 123.

[53] Apollodorus, *The Library, 2.4.12,* pp 72-73.

8) **Steal the herd of wild, man-eating Mares** of Thracian King Diomedes, a son of Ares.
9) Confiscate the belt of Hippolyta, queen of the Amazons, and daughter of the war god Ares.
10) **Steal the cattle** of the three-bodied man Geryon.
11) **Snatch three golden apples** from the nymphs called the Hesperides.
12) **Trap the three-headed hound Cerberus**, who supposedly guarded the gates of Hades.[54]

As Apollodorus describes it, Heracles "received a sword from Hermes, a bow and arrows from Apollo, a golden breastplate from Hephaistos, and a robe from Athena; and he cut a club for himself at Nemea."[55]

Gaia and the Great Goddess

In Greek mythology, Gaia is a crucial primal component of origins, though not alone. According to Hesiod, in the beginning was Chaos, then came Gaia (earth), along with Eros (procreation). Gaia brought forth Ouranos (sky) and they mated to create the first generation of gods called the Titans, as explained earlier.

Greek scholar Robin Hard explains that though Gaia is often described in personal terms, she was never fully realized as an anthropomorphic being like other gods, such as Zeus or Hera. This is most likely because she was that physical home that gave life to all living creatures, including humans. But because of this nurturing character she was called "Mother of All," "the eldest of all beings who nourishes all living creatures and brings prosperity to the human race through her harvests and the livestock that she supports."[56]

---

54 Apollodorus, *The Library, 2.5,* pp 73-84.

55 Apollodorus, *The Library, 2.4.11,* p 72.

56 Robin Hard, *The Routledge Handbook of Greek Mythology, 8th edition* (Oxon, OX: Routledge, 1928, 2020), 22.

There is a history of some classical scholars since the mid-nineteenth century arguing for what historian Cynthia Eller calls the myth of matriarchal pre-history. This is the belief that ancient humanity's original religion before writing's invention (and therefore, "pre-historical") was that of "the Great Goddess," where the feminine ruled agrarian society and women were revered as priestesses of the Goddess and sources of peace and cultural nurture. But then, at some point, men overthrew this Matriarchy utopia and replaced it with the Patriarchy warrior society, a domination of male rule that leads to the "evils" of female subordination, disharmony between the sexes and society, and ultimately war. They pine for a return to worship of the Great Goddess that would return us to harmony within humanity and with the earth (Gaia).[57]

Though many modern neo-pagans and feminists of the "Goddess Movement" consider Gaia a popular representative for this matriarchal mythology, they often consider the Great Goddess as a sublime incorporation of many of the world's goddesses. Some academics have argued for either Hera or Athena as the original Great Goddess because they were the patron deities of Greece's two oldest cities, Argos and Athens.[58]

Eller debunks this modern myth as a feminist cultural projection with certainly no manuscript support (it was pre-history after all) and a dismal lack of artifactual evidence:

> There is also nothing in the archaeological record that is at odds with an image of prehistoric life as nasty, brutish, short, and male-dominated.... And whatever religions prehistoric peoples practiced, we can be fairly sure that goddess worship did not automatically yield cultures of

---

[57] Cynthia Eller, *The Myth of Matriarchal Prehistory: Why an Invented Past Won't Give Women a Future* (Boston: Beacon Press, 2001), 3.

[58] H. D. F. Kitto, *The Greeks* (England: Penguin Books, 1951-1967), 18.

peace and plenty led by the goddess's priestesses. This pattern has been found nowhere.[59]

Poseidon

After the Olympians defeated the Titans, one of Zeus's two brothers, Poseidon, had been allotted not merely the sea as his domain but also power over the elements that affected the earth, such as storms and earthquakes, the latter of which gave him the epithet "Earth-shaker." He was also a patron deity of horses.[60]

Though Poseidon's consort was the sea nymph Amphitrite, he was sexual promiscuous like his brother Zeus, coupling with both male and female, divine and human, willing and unwilling. He is described as being highly competitive for the control of cities and was famous for losing Athens to the goddess Athena but still maintaining a presence there.[61]

One of his conquests was raping Demeter, the fertility goddess of agriculture and harvest. Because she had tried to escape by turning into a horse, Poseidon turned into a stallion to find her.[62] Related to this, Poseidon was a patron deity of horses.[63] The winged horse Pegasus was one of his offspring.

Hades and Persephone

Pluto, Zeus's eldest brother, was allotted the underworld as his supreme domain after imprisoning the Titans in Tartarus. His name in the classical Greek tradition was Hades, but by the Hellenistic era, Hades became known as the name for the underworld itself, and the god's name was renamed Pluto.

---

59 Eller, *The Myth of Matriarchal Prehistory*, 181.

60 Hard, *The Routledge Handbook*, 125.

61 Kitto, *The Greeks*, 14.

62 Pausanias, *Description of Greece*, 8.25.5.

63 Hard, *The Routledge Handbook*, 125.

Hades was well known for his abduction, rape, and forced marriage of Persephone, a vegetation goddess, daughter of Zeus and Demeter. As the goddess of agriculture, Demeter cursed the earth with famine until Zeus ordered Hades to allow Persephone to return to her mother. Hades, however, gave Persephone food to eat from the underworld that tied her to it, requiring she return for at least a third of every year, which corresponded to the agricultural seasonal cycle.[64]

Hades' domain, Hades, was the Greek equivalent of the Hebrew concept Sheol. Hades/Sheol was not a synonym for the fiery place of punishment for sins known as Hell. Hades/Sheol was considered the underworld place where the spirits of both the righteous and unrighteous dead go.

---

[64] Apollodorus, *The Library,* 1.5, pp. 33-34. "Hymn 2 to Demeter": Anonymous. *The Homeric Hymns and Homerica with an English Translation* by Hugh G. Evelyn-White. Homeric Hymns. Cambridge, MA: Harvard University Press; London, William Heinemann Ltd., 1914.

Chapter 5
Greek Gods in the New Testament

Though the *Judah Maccabee* novels take place in the Intertestamental time period, this was only two hundred years before the New Testament-era of Gospel expansion through the Apostles, as laid out in the book of Acts. It should be no surprise therefore that there are reflections of Greek spiritual influence even to that day. Of course, the New Testament speaks of subverting those influences with the power of the Gospel. So let's take a look at a few of those vestiges that remained from Daniel's third beast kingdom, the kingdom of the Greeks.

Logos

The Gospel of John opens with a famous doctrinal statement pregnant with meaning:

> John 1:1–3
> In the beginning was the Word, and the Word was with God, and the Word was God. He was in the beginning with God. All things were made through him, and without him was not anything made that was made.

As most Christians know, the Greek word for *Word* in this text is *logos*. And it carries far more meaning than its common English usage, as in words in sentences. The Apostle John is subverting a Greek concept prevalent in his day. In the ancient world, all cultures and worldviews were rooted in religious beliefs. Sure, there have always been unbelievers who might cynically use that system to their benefit or sometimes openly stand against the crowd. But it was the Greek world that brought an emphasis on reason and philosophical discourse that would ultimately expand to dominate the modern world in which we now live.

Ancient Greek philosophy has traditionally been understood to begin in the sixth century BC with the rise of the "Pre-Socratic" philosophers. Several schools and individuals rose to prominence as they developed their understanding of the universe through a systematic lens of reason, mathematics, and a primitive version of science. They sought to discover permanent principles and laws behind the universe as they understood it. One of these philosophers, Heraclitus, coined the term *Logos* as a reference to the underlying order or structure of the universe. There was nevertheless still a mysterious divine identity behind it.

Next came the philosophical era known as Classical Greek, headed by such luminaries as Socrates, Plato, and Aristotle. As philosophy developed, various thinkers like Plato retained a belief in deities, but the universal acid of logic and the search for the laws behind the cosmos's workings stripped the need for a deity in the minds of many Greeks. If one could understand the order of things, what need was there for gods?

By the time of Hellenism, multiple schools of thought between Plato and Aristotle competed for dominance. Some of the most popular schools rose to last even into the New Testament era. Two of these were Epicureanism and Stoicism. Of the two, Stoicism became known for its materialist theory of the Logos as the underlying Reason, Fate, or God behind all things. They used the term "god," or even "Zeus" interchangeably with Logos, but in the end, such usage could be seen as accommodation to the popular beliefs in the gods just as much as a subversive push away from them. Logos was Reason was God was Zeus. But it was just materialistic fate in the Stoic mind. Thus the common description of the Stoic person who could accept the unchanging laws of fate with a kind of resolute indifference despite it all. A kind of unreasoned resistance to their own logical conclusions of reason.

But of course, even within this materialist paradigm, the notion of divinity or transcendence lurks with an inescapable persistence of necessity. After all, nature's regularity or "law-likeness" presupposes a transcendent Creator that sustains the order. Otherwise, everything is, at its foundation random chaos, and order is an illusion. Yet definitionally, order transcends the chaos of the cosmos.

Thus, the notion of divinity continued to lurk beneath Greek philosophy's mysterious Logos. But because of its materialist construct, the Logos was, by definition, abstract and impersonal.

So when the Apostle John equates the Christian God with the Logos, he is actually drawing upon that Greek intellectual pursuit of the cosmos's underlying order. The Logos/Zeus in Stoic thought permeated everything and was the spark of divinity found in all human beings. The Apostle Paul also dealt with this Logos/Zeus belief in Acts 17, where he debates the Athenian philosophers on the Areopagus. He even quotes Stoic authors in agreement that "in him [Zeus] we live and move and have our being" and that "we are indeed his [Zeus's] offspring" (Acts 17:28).

Now, the Stoics whom Paul quotes, from Aratus to Cleanthes, were clearly referring to Zeus as the Logos. Aratus writes, "Let us begin with Zeus…for we are truly his offspring" and "Almighty Zeus…we who live and creep upon the earth are all thy children."[1] Paul's entire sermon to the Athenians agrees with their notions of the Logos not dwelling in "temples built by man," of determining "allotted periods and boundaries of their dwelling," and of being "not far from us."[2] Paul even declares that, despite their philosophy, Greeks are still a very religious people because of their belief in the Logos (Acts 17:22).

So both Paul and John are consciously using the Stoic understanding of Zeus/Logos to define Jesus/Yahweh. Does this mean that the Apostles agreed with Greek Stoics by saying that their God was *identical with* Zeus/Logos? Absolutely not. Both apostles actually engage in *subverting* the Greek Logos. They appeal to some common

---

[1] Aratus (c. 315-239 B.C.E.) Phaenomena, Lines 1-16; see F. F. Bruce, *The Book of the Acts,* New International Commentary on the New Testament, rev. ed. (Grand Rapids, MI: Eerdmans, 1988), 337-339.

[2] For a detailed exploration of Acts 17 and its subversion of Stoic beliefs, see Brian Godawa, *God Against the gods: Storytelling, Imagination & Apologetics in the Bible* (Allen, TX: Warrior Poet Publishing, 2016, 2021), 101-118.

notions of Zeus/Logos, only to turn around and tell them that the Greeks are following the *wrong* god. They have missed the real truth undergirding their beliefs. Just a few verses after John tells how the Logos created all things, he writes, "And the Word [Logos] became flesh and dwelt among us, and we have seen his glory, glory as of the only Son from the Father" (John 1:14; 1 John 1:1-3). The Stoic Logos was an impersonal force of fate. They only called it Zeus to subvert their own people away from Greece's more personal gods. They found the concept of a God becoming a human philosophically repugnant.

And Paul would do the same with the Athenians on Areopagus at his sermon's conclusion. He would also say that the deity they called Logos was actually unknown to them. But Paul said that he personally knew for whom they groped blindly (Acts 17:23, 27). And that very Creator appointed a man [Jesus] to judge the world by raising him from the dead (Acts 17:31). The Greeks would also find this repulsive because they believed no man could be the ultimate judge, and since no man had ever returned from Hades, as Aeschylus wrote, "there is no resurrection."[3]

So the New Testament Apostles were overthrowing the Greek divine Logos by redefining him through Gospel proclamation to be a infinite person of the triune Godhead who became flesh and rose from the dead. That is how Jesus/Yahweh triumphs over Zeus/Logos.

Artemis

In Acts 19:21-41, Luke tells the story of Paul preaching the Gospel in Ephesus, where the cult of the Greek goddess Artemis was strong. It was home of a great temple to Artemis and many idols of the goddess were bought and sold there. Artemis, the city's patron deity, was considered the mother goddess of fertility childbirth and of wildlife. Closely related to Cybele, the Greeks considered her the mother goddess of Asia Minor and a chief deity of the Amazonian tribe of

[3] Aeschylus, *Eumenides,* 647.

women warriors. Bible commentator Clinton Arnold describes this powerful religious center of Artemis:

> Her grand temple in Ephesus was lauded by ancient writers as one of the Seven Wonders of the World. The structure of the cult was integrally interwoven into the fabric of daily life and culture. The temple functioned as the banking and financial center for the province. Large amounts of money were deposited and borrowed from the Artemision. The cult also owned substantial amounts of property in the area. … The worshipers of Artemis regarded her as supreme among all the gods and goddesses.[4]

Big Idol Worship was big money. When Paul persuaded many of the citizens that these "things made with hands are not gods" (19:26), it severely disrupted the idol makers' economy. One of them, Demetrius, warned the Ephesians that this would depose the Great Artemis "from her magnificence" (19:27). It caused a riot in the city where many idol worshippers yelled, "Great is Artemis of the Ephesians!" (19:28, 34). It took a town clerk with strong legal reasoning to quiet them down and use due process of law if they desired justice.

Though there is no outright spiritual warfare depicted here, it certainly captures the hostility toward the Gospel living in the idol worshippers' hearts. But there was another location of Paul's preaching that elicited a spiritual reaction from demons: Philippi.

Python Spirit

In Acts 16:16-24, we read about Paul with Silas, Luke, and others visiting the city of Philippi in Macedonia. I will let Luke relate the basic opening:

---

4 Clinton E. Arnold, Acts, ed. Clinton E. Arnold, vol. 2B, *Zondervan Illustrated Bible Backgrounds Commentary* (Grand Rapids, MI: Zondervan, 2002), 198.

> Acts 16:16–18
> As we were going to the place of prayer, we were met by a slave girl who had a **spirit of divination ["python spirit"]** and brought her owners much gain by fortune-telling. She followed Paul and us, crying out, "These men are servants of the Most High God, who proclaim to you the way of salvation." And this she kept doing for many days. Paul, having become greatly annoyed, turned and said to the spirit, "I command you in the name of Jesus Christ to come out of her." And it came out that very hour.

In this passage as well, there was big money in idolatry. But don't let the money motive blind you to the fact that, in the biblical worldview, the "spirit of divination" was a demonic reality. In a Greek religious context, the spirit of the Python serpent was related to Apollo and the oracle of Delphi in Greece. Commentator Clinton Arnold explains:

> The Python dragon or serpent was associated with the oracle sanctuary at Delphi, about eighty miles northwest of Athens. In the story of the origin of the cult, Apollo killed this large snake that was guarding the entrance to the oracle cave. Apollo then became the guardian and patron of this sanctuary, which was an entrance to the underworld. During the Greco-Roman era, people came from all over the Mediterranean world to consult the priestesses of Apollo (called *pythia*) for advice. The Pythia descended into the oracle grotto to seek inspiration from the god by allowing herself to be possessed by a spirit. She then arose and uttered the god's instructions to the inquirer—first in an ecstatic, gibberish speech and then typically in the form of Greek verse.[5]

I depict Pythia priestesses in the *Judah Maccabee* novels. Like the book of Acts, I have some that exist outside of Delphi, all the way over in Antioch. But there was another divination element peculiar to the Oracle

---

[5] Clinton E. Arnold, *Acts,* ed. Clinton E. Arnold, vol. 2B, Zondervan Illustrated Bible Backgrounds Commentary (Grand Rapids, MI: Zondervan, 2002), 157.

of Delphi: drug use. Many classical authors have attested to observations of the temple, where Pythia priestesses sat on chairs placed over natural crevices from which strange vapors ascended, resulting in "a divine state of possession."[6] Conveniently, Delphi was situated in an actively volcanic area. Recent archaeology has uncovered traces of hydrocarbon gases in the soil and water near the temple which point to the possibility of volcanic releases factoring in the intoxicating Pythian visions.

In the Bible, the Greek word for *sorcery* is *pharmakeia*, from which we get our word *pharmacy*. While this is not an indictment of all drugs, it shows that some usage of certain drugs can serve as portals through which one could actually contact demonic spirits. Fortunately, the power in the name of Jesus Christ cast the demon out of the little girl in this Acts story. But unfortunately, this resulted in another city-wide disturbance that led to a mob beating Paul and his companions with rods and throwing them into prison with their feet in stocks. Idol worshippers do not like their lucrative demonic spirits being overthrown so easily. But again, the power of Greek gods is nothing compared to the power of our God.

And this brings me to the next notion of the Greek gods in the New Testament. According to the Apostle Paul, the demonic beings are real.

Gods as Demons

In 1 Corinthians chapters 8 and 10, the Apostle Paul addresses the Church regarding eating food sacrificed to idols. In that world, markets and homes cooked food to eat that was often offered before the images or idols of gods before offering it to patrons or visitors to consume. Some Christians believed that to eat such food constituted unfaithfulness to Jesus as Lord. Others believed the idols had no power over food since Jesus was the creator of food and the supreme Lord over the gods. Paul's answer was to find truth in both sides.

---

[6] From the geographer Strabo (c. 64 BC-25 AD) as quoted in Jelle Zeilinga de Boer and John R. Hale, "The Oracle of Delphi—Was She Really Stoned?" *Bible History Daily*, May 2013. https://www.biblicalarchaeology.org/daily/ancient-cultures/daily-life-and-practice/the-oracle-of-delphi-was-she-really-stoned/#end02 (retrieved October 30, 2024).

In Corinth, the number of Greek gods worshipped was manifold. Aphrodite, the goddess of love and beauty, was one of Corinth's principal deities. She had a prominent temple on the Acropolis that included temple prostitution for the populace. Apollo also had a temple in the agora, or marketplace, that was one of the city's oldest structures. As a port city, Corinth honored Poseidon, god of the sea. Mystery rites were performed there for Demeter and Persephone, goddesses of the harvest, and festivals for Dionysus the god of wine, fertility, and revelry were celebrated yearly. When it came to sacrificial offering, there were plenty of gods from which the Corinthians could choose.

Here are the two passages where Paul addresses the debate:

> 1 Corinthians 8:4–6
> Therefore, as to the eating of food offered to idols, we know that "an idol has no real existence," and that "there is no God but one." **For although there may be so-called gods in heaven or on earth—as indeed there are many "gods"** and many "lords"—yet for us there is one God, the Father.

> 1 Corinthians 10:18–21
> Consider the people of Israel: are not those who eat the sacrifices participants in the altar? What do I imply then? That food offered to idols is anything, or that an idol is anything? No, I imply that **what pagans sacrifice they offer to demons and not to God**. I do not want you to be participants with demons. You cannot drink the cup of the Lord and the cup of demons. You cannot partake of the table of the Lord and the table of demons.

Some Christians will point to statements in chapter 8, like "an idol has no real existence" or "there is no God but one," as indicating absolute monotheism where these pagan deities are mere imaginary fictions. No other gods exist other than Yahweh/Jesus.

But when one takes a closer look at the passages, this argument dissolves into contradiction. Remember earlier, we established that the

Hebrew understanding of gods was that angels from God's heavenly host are called "gods" (Hebrew: *elohim*, Greek: *theos*) in some places (e.g., Job 38:4-7).[7] So the cosmos, or world order, of the Hebrew worldview included created beings that were not infinite, all-knowing, and eternal creators, but who existed as divine beings in the spiritual plane, called "gods."

So when Paul claims in 1 Corinthians 8 that the "idol" or image has no real existence, he uses the word *cosmos* behind that English translation of "existence." They believed idols represented the presence of the deity on earth upon performance of a ritual called "opening of the mouth."[8] The idol would receive the deity's breath as its presence. According to Paul, this worldview had no place in the Christian biblical cosmos or worldview.

When Paul says "there is no God but one," he is referring to the Shema of Israel that declares, "Hear, O Israel: Yahweh our God, Yahweh is one" (Deuteronomy 6:4). Paul immediately clarifies that even though there are many gods being worshipped, *for us* there is one God. That is, God's people worship only one God. He is not saying there are no other gods, but that Christians worship only one God, Yahweh. This is the true form of biblical monotheism, not polytheism or henotheism.

When Paul calls the gods "so-called," this is not calling them fictions, because right after this he clarifies, "indeed there are many gods" (8:5). He is referring to their lack of authority in the believer's life in comparison with Yahweh's. Chapter 10 gives the final context to this meaning by claiming that the pagan gods are actually demons. They are a spiritual reality behind the idols. The idols are nothing. They are wood and stone and silver. But the spiritual beings *behind those idols* are real and they are demons. This is where he suggests that some participation in eating the food may be participation with demons. He

---

7 See also Psalm 82:1, 6 with John 10:33-36.

8 Edward Mason Curtis, *Man as the Image of God in Genesis in the Light of Ancient Near Eastern Parallels* (Dissertation, University of Pennsylvania, 1984), 100-102.

reaffirms the idol is nothing in relation to the cosmos, but the demons behind them are real.

The phrase that Paul uses in chapter 10, "what pagans sacrifice they offer to demons and not to God," is the veil pulled back on what he means about pagan Gods. This statement is almost certainly an allusion to (if not a paraphrased quote of) Deuteronomy 32, where Yahweh calls the gods of Canaan that the Israelites were worshipping *demons*. And demons are real spiritual beings, not imaginary fictional ones.

> Deuteronomy 32:17 (NASB95)
> "They [Israelites] sacrificed to **demons who were not God,**
> **To gods** whom they have not known,
> New gods who came lately,
> Whom your fathers did not dread.

This concept is echoed elsewhere in the Old Testament as well:

> Leviticus 17:7
> So they shall no more sacrifice their sacrifices to **goat demons**, after whom they whore.

The Hebrew word translated here as "goat demons" is *seirim*, which is the plural of *satyrs*, the hybrid half-goat/half-human deity.[9]

> Psalm 106:37–38
> They [Israelites] sacrificed their sons and their daughters **to the demons [satyrs]**; they poured out innocent blood, the blood of their sons and daughters, whom they sacrificed to **the idols of Canaan**, and the land was polluted with blood.

[9] See also 2 Chronicles 11:15; Isaiah 13:21, 34:14.

> Psalm 95:5-6 (LXX)
> For great is the Lord, and praiseworthy exceedingly. More awesome he is than all the gods. For **all the gods of the nations are demons**, but the Lord made the heavens."[10]

We see in these passages that pagan gods were considered demons. But they were real beings behind those images (idols) called "gods" (*elohim, theos*). When Paul calls the pagan deities "so-called" gods he is not saying they do not exist, but only that *compared to Yahweh,* the God of gods, they are without authority. Demons have no power in the face of Jesus. "So-called gods" in chapter 8 is a phrase of comparative quality, not of non-existence. In the New Testament, the pagan "gods of the nations," as in Psalm 95 and Deuteronomy 32 above, were the principalities and powers over territories, not fictions or metaphors as the modern materialist mind conceives them.

Zeus again

Acts 14:8-18 relates the story of Paul and Barnabas preaching in Lystra, a Roman colony. After Paul heals a man crippled from birth, the residents misinterpret the act and conclude that Paul and Barnabas were the Greek gods Zeus and Hermes come to earth "in the likeness of men" (14:11). They were most likely drawing upon local legends by the first-century Roman poet Ovid who wrote about the king of the gods, Zeus, and his speaker, Hermes, visiting Phrygia looking for hospitality under the guise of mortals. A thousand homes rejected them until an elderly couple named Philemon and Baucis accepted them. As Clinton Arnold describes the story,

> The old couple welcomed the two visitors, fed them well, and prepared for them a place to rest. Not knowing that they were entertaining gods "in the guise of human

[10] Randall Tan, David A. deSilva, and Logos Bible Software. *The Lexham Greek-English Interlinear Septuagint.* Logos Bible Software, 2009. Baruch 4:7 in the Apocrypha echoes this Scriptural theme as well when speaking of Israel's apostasy: "For you provoked him who made you, by sacrificing to demons and not to God."

> beings," the old couple finally learned the identity of their heavenly visitors. The gods then led Philemon and Baucis to the top of a hill and mercifully spared them from a devastating flood sent in judgment on the inhospitable inhabitants of the region. Their humble home was miraculously transformed into a marble temple.[11]

It is easy to see why the local priest of Zeus then wanted to offer sacrifices to Paul and Barnabas, who reasoned with them that they were only but men, like the Lystrians, and should repent from idols to worship the living God (14:15). But the grip of delusion was so strong on those people that even Paul's words "scarcely restrained the people from offering sacrifices to them" (14:18).

Though there is no supernatural element to this story, it reinforces the idea that Greek gods were still a stronghold in the Roman empire during the propagation of the Gospel.

But there is a simple Bible verse that references Zeus with a more supernatural angle. Let's take a look at it.

And Zeus Again

Revelation 2:13 reveals Jesus's prophetic words to the church of Pergamum (or Pergamon) in the first century AD:

> Revelation 2:12–13
> "And to the angel of the church in Pergamum write: 'The words of him who has the sharp two-edged sword. "I know where you dwell, **where Satan's throne is**. Yet you hold fast my name, and you did not deny my faith even in the days of Antipas my faithful witness, who was killed among you, **where Satan dwells**.'""

Most Bible commentators acknowledge that this section of Revelation is addressed to seven historical, first-century churches that

---

[11] From Ovid, *Metamorphoses* 8.618-724. Clinton E. Arnold, *Acts*, ed. Clinton E. Arnold, vol. 2B, Zondervan Illustrated Bible Backgrounds Commentary (Grand Rapids, MI: Zondervan, 2002), 133.

existed on a postal route in Asia Minor when John wrote the letter. The Holy Spirit gives blessing and warning to each church in light of the momentous world-changing events in their near future.

But regardless of one's eschatological system, the historical city of Pergamum was known for being a center of Roman government and religion in Asia Minor in the first century. It was one of the first cities to build a temple to Augustus, the first emperor to initiate the imperial cult of Caesar as divine. The current Caesar was persecuting Christians, so it would be easy to call him Satan, God's ultimate adversary. But as New Testament scholar G.K. Beale writes,

> The reference to "Satan's throne" may also have been brought to mind because of the conical hill behind Pergamum which was the site of many temples, prominent among which was the throne-like altar of Zeus, which itself would have been sufficient to arouse the thought of the devil's throne.[12]

This throne of Zeus was so famous that despite its loss to history, a replica was built and now stands in the Pergamon Museum in Berlin, Germany. Large marble friezes atop the altar depict engravings of the Gigantomachy battle between the Olympians and the Giants of Greek myth.

Now the name Satan in the text is more precisely "the *satan*," which denotes a job title, "the adversary" of God, thus fitting for either Caesar or Zeus. But there is good reason to consider The Adversary as taking on an individual ontological status in the text of Revelation. John links the great dragon of his vision with "that ancient serpent, who is called the devil and the *satan*, the deceiver of the whole world—he was thrown down to the earth, and his angels were thrown down with him" (Revelation 12:9). Satan is the *satan*. The Adversary has become incarnate.

---

[12] G. K. Beale, *The Book of Revelation: A Commentary on the Greek Text,* New International Greek Testament Commentary (Grand Rapids, MI; Carlisle, Cumbria: W.B. Eerdmans; Paternoster Press, 1999), 246.

The conclusion here would be that Zeus was called Satan, thus giving him some spiritual reality or connection to the spiritual ruler over Pergamum. Satan "dwelled there" in Pergamum as Zeus, and Zeus's throne was in fact a throne of Satan. This connection was more than metaphor or analogy. It carried the weight of spiritual being.

Chapter 6
Temples and Cosmic Mountains

One of the key thematic elements of the story of the Maccabees is the cleansing of the Jerusalem temple from the Abomination of Desolation, the altar to Zeus, which inspired the Jewish festival of Hanukkah. One reason for this is the central position that the holy temple has in biblical theology from Old Covenant to New Covenant. Its roots go deep to the underworld and its ceiling reaches to the heavens. Like Enoch's celestial journey, let's travel through some connections to get a taste of God's incredible meaning embedded in these cosmic images in Scripture.

The Garden

First off, the temple and its precursor, the tabernacle in the wilderness, are both incarnate pictures of the Garden of Eden within the heavens and earth. It is important to remember that Yahweh gave the blueprint of the tabernacle directly to Moses (Exodus 25:9), so the details are not arbitrary but of heavenly significance. Thus, Solomon's subsequent temple was an adapted version of that blueprint that maintained much of the same imagery. Solomon's temple was destroyed in the Babylonian Exile in the 6th century BC and, at the end of that century, Zerubbabel built a second temple, which King Herod later expanded and completed in the first century AD. Ironically the temple was then destroyed in AD 70, within a generation of being completed—never to be rebuilt. The New Testament Apostles then explain that with the coming of Jesus Messiah, the temple was ultimately reconstituted spiritually in Jesus and physically on earth in the body of Christ (Ephesians 2:19-22).[1]

If we work our way inward from the temple's outer courtyard into the Holy of Holies, we can more distinctly see the cosmos paradigm as a picture of one coming closer to God's presence. The temple's outer courtyard where citizens could assemble was called the Court of Gentiles. This corresponded to the wide world outside of God's Garden.

As one entered the "Beautiful Gate," the final courtyard began to exhibit garden imagery that would increase as one entered the temple building. This inner courtyard featured the stone altar of sacrifice as well as the large bronze basin where the priests would wash themselves in executing their duties. The bronze basin, called "the sea," rested on the backs of twelve engraved oxen. The basin's lip was to be carved like an open lily and ornamented with gourds (1 Kings 7:23-26). The altar of sacrifice, originally an "altar of earth" in the days of the tabernacle (Exodus 20:24-25), was, in Solomon's day, made of rock untouched by human tools. Together, these symbolized the earth and sea of God's creation.

There were also twelve bronze basin stands that had panels featuring more engraved animals and vegetation: cherubim, lions, and palm trees (1 Kings 7:36). When one entered between the two huge bronze pillars of the temple entrance, they walked beneath engravings of hundreds of pomegranates and lilies on the latticework above (7:18-22).

The inner temple consisted of two chambers, the Holy Place, representing the Garden of Eden, and the Most Holy Place, representing the very throne of Yahweh in that paradise. Now, the garden imagery explodes all over the place to reinforce this inner sanctum as a sacred symbol of the Garden of Eden as God's own throne.

Here is a list of some of the temple's ornamentation that featured garden imagery:

---

[1] See also 1 Corinthians 3:16-17; 2 Corinthians 6:16; Hebrews 3:6; 1 Timothy 3:15; and 1 Peter 2:4-10.

• The walls of the inner temple were cedar wood carved with the forms of gourds and open flowers (6:18).

• More cherubim engraved on all the interior walls, along with palm trees and open flowers (6:29).

• More cherubim, palm trees, and open flowers engraved on the doors to the inner sanctuary (6:31).

• More cherubim, palm trees, and open flowers engraved on the doors to the nave (6:33).

• The gold menorah lampstand in the Holy Place, an obvious symbol of the Tree of Life in the Garden, was crafted as an almond tree with blossoms and flowers on its seven branches (Exodus 37:19-21). Some have even claimed that the seven lights represented the seven major lights in the sky (five planets and the sun and moon).

• The veil to the Most Holy Place was covered with embroidered images of cherubim (2 Chronicles 3:14).

• Two gold-gilded cherubim in the Most Holy Place (6:23-28) hearkened back to the cherubim guarding Eden (Genesis 3:24).

The priests caring for the temple represented Adam, who was responsible to care for the Garden. Scholar G. K. Beale points out that the two Hebrew words used throughout the Old Testament (e.g., Numbers 3:7-8 and 1 Chronicles 23:32) for the priestly duties to "cultivate and keep" the tabernacle and, later, the temple, are the same two Hebrew words describing Adam's responsibility to "cultivate and keep" the Garden in Genesis 2:15. He concludes that, "the writer of Genesis 2 was portraying Adam against the later portrait of Israel's priests, and that he was the archetypal priest who served in and guarded (or 'took care of') God's first temple."[2]

So the temple, as an image of the Garden of Eden, operated as a sequence of sacred spaces that came closer and closer to the very presence of God in his throne room in that Garden. The performance of sacrifices operated on the spiritual level of returning the worshippers to the presence of God from which mankind, in Adam, had originally been kicked out. The sacrificial system was a return to Eden, a temporary overcoming of the Garden expulsion until Messiah would come.

This is why the Jews considered placing an altar to a pagan god like Zeus in the temple was an abomination of desolation. The Hebrew word for *desolation* had to do with making a place deserted. The presence of an idol in Yahweh's temple meant Yahweh would desert that place because he would tolerate no gods beside him. So if his people tolerated such abominations, then Yahweh's presence would be far from that location. In a way, the Maccabees cleansed the temple to make it fit for Yahweh to return, and he did return in Messiah two hundred years later (Matthew 21:33-45; 22:1-14).

The temple of God is also called the "house of God" (Daniel 1:2; Matthew 12:4). But there is another theological element tied to the holy temple and Eden imagery explored in the *Judah Maccabee* novels, and that is the cosmic mountain.

The Cosmic Mountain

Most religions of the ancient Near East and around the world believed humans met with gods on mountains. Many also reside in tents or temples (their "houses") constructed on mountains, both natural and man-made. The Olympian gods of Greece were well known to live on Mount Olympus within a great palace. The storm god of Canaan, Ba'al,

---

[2] G. K. Beale, *The Temple and the Church's Mission: A Biblical Theology of the Dwelling Place of God*, ed. D. A. Carson, vol. 17, New Studies in Biblical Theology (Downers Grove, IL; England: InterVarsity Press; Apollos, 2004), 68.

lived in his house on Mount Zaphon (or Sapan) in Syria's northern heights. The Canaanite high god El had his abode on Mount Hermon in Lebanon.[3] Iconography of Hittite religion illustrate some crossover with their gods, like Teshub standing on divine mountains such as Zaphon and Mount Hermon.[4] Sumerian mythology describes the goddess Inanna, known as the "Queen of heaven," as "dwelling on the peaks of bright mountains."[5]

A few of these cosmic mountains come into play in the *Judah Maccabee* novels and in my entire series of Chronicles novels, in particular, Mount Olympus, Mount Zaphon, and Mount Hermon, about which we will explore more in a moment.

And if there was not a natural mountain at hand, humans would construct one for their gods to come down and dwell in their midst. The most ancient Tower of Babel in Genesis 11 is now known to have been a ziggurat, a step-pyramid that served as a step-ladder to heaven, the top of which housed a temple where they claimed gods came down and met man, who climbed up to meet them. When the text says that the Tower of Babel had its "top in the heavens" (Genesis 11:4) this was not a reference to its height so much as its purpose of being a sacred space where the gods from heaven would "come down" and meet with man. Genesis 11:5 uses the phrase of Yahweh "coming down" to see the tower as a veiled reference to him subverting the gods, stepping in, and displacing them with his presence to judge the idolaters.

Their creators considered ziggurats to be holy mountains, a concept which exists in ancient religious cultures worldwide, from China to Mesopotamia to Egypt to South America.

---

3 Lipinski, Edward. "El's Abode: Mythological Traditions Related to Mount Hermon and to the Mountains of Armenia," (*Orientalia Lovaniensa Periodica 2*, 1971), 13-69.

4 Richard J. Clifford, *The Cosmic Mountain in Canaan and the Old Testament* (Cambridge, MA: Harvard University Press, 1972), 32.

5 Amar Annus, "The Story of the Watchers as Counternarrative: the Relevance of Babylonian Apocrypha to Enochic Traditions," published in *Proceedings of the Conference on the Enochic Chronotope*, Berlin, December 2013, p. 13.

Another theological element of mountains is not only that they connect heaven and earth but that they can also be doorways to the underworld in the eyes of the ancients. The Ba'al Cycle describes the Canaanite high god El's mountain abode as descending to the underworld dwelling of Mot, the god of death.[6] In the Bible, we see the same concept of mountains connected with the underworld. Mount Peor was the location in Moab where the Israelites, before crossing into the Promised Land, engaged in the idolatrous Moabite Cult of the Dead (Psalm 106:28). The name of the mountain, Peor, has been connected with the open mouth of Sheol, the Hebrew term for the underworld.[7]

In the prophecy against God's spiritual enemy Gog, Ezekiel claims that on the day of God's judgment of Gog, Yahweh "will give to Gog a place for burial in Israel, the Valley of the Travelers [*oberim*], east of the sea. It will block the travelers [*oberim*], for there Gog and all his multitude will be buried" (Ezekiel 39:11).

This prophecy's supernatural aspect is obscured by the English translation. The Hebrew word for *travelers* in the text, *oberim*, is actually a word that refers to contacting the spirits of the dead who are traveling or "crossing over" into the underworld. This makes sense in the context of God's judgment of death upon Gog's demonic army. God would block the natural crossing over of the dead spirits of Gog's army because of their evil done against Israel. And this spiritual judgment takes place in a valley—*at the base of a mountain*. Mountain tops are connection points between heaven and earth and its roots connect the earth and the underworld.

This all becomes clearer when one understands that the God of the Bible uses the same method of interacting with humanity. He, too, manifests himself in temples on mountains. Remember when I explained above that the Jerusalem temple was a symbolic image of the

---

[6] Clifford, *The Cosmic Mountain*, 79-80.

[7] Klaas Spronk, *Beatific Afterlife in Ancient Israel and in the Ancient Near East* (Germany: Verlag Butzon & Bercker Kevelaer), 229.

Garden of Eden? Well, that Garden and that temple *were both on mountains*.

In a famous passage of Ezekiel 28, Yahweh laments over the prideful king of Tyre and proclaims judgment against him. Though many Christians speculate that this passage has a hidden meaning that refers to the fall of the *satan* in the garden, all Bible scholars agree that its primary direct application is to an earthly king whom Babylonian invaders would eventually overthrow. However one draws their analogy, the passage surely uses Eden as a metaphor for the glorious city of Tyre over which the king ruled. And my main interest here is that Eden is described as being "on the holy mountain of God" (Ezekiel 28:14, 16). The Garden of Eden was on a mountain!

Now, when we learn that the temple in Jerusalem is described as being on Mount Zion, it makes more sense than mere geographical description. Though Jerusalem is not a huge mountain like Zaphon or Hermon, it is surely an elevated land mass, symbolically called Mount Zion. Although the meaning of the name Zion is unclear, it is sometimes used of the city and sometimes of the temple mount. But as the *Anchor Bible Dictionary* explains,

> The temple is therefore also called Zion, Mt. Zion, or the holy hill of Zion. The divine King of Israel is frequently spoken of as dwelling there. God, the Lord, is said to be enthroned in Zion (Ps 9:10); it (the temple) is his dwelling place (Ps 76:1), his holy hill (Joel 4:17, cf. the glory of God on the tabernacle, Exod 40:34). The Lord Almighty, is dwelling on Mt. Zion (Isa 8:18). God shines forth from Zion (Ps 50:2), the place where his Name dwells (Isa 18:7). It is from Zion that a deliverer/redeemer will come forth (Rom 11:26a [= Isa 59:20a]). This deliverer is the Son of

> whom God speaks, "I have installed my King on Zion, my holy hill" (Ps 2:6).[8]

Prior to building his house on his holy cosmic mountain of Zion in Jerusalem, Yahweh first revealed himself to Moses and the Israelites escaping Egypt at Mount Sinai. Though the tabernacle was not on the mountain but at its base, God nevertheless pitched the original tent at his first holy mountain.

So the Bible's narrative involves God creating his first temple, the Garden of Eden, on a mountain. This temple is reimagined in the tabernacle near Mount Sinai, then solidified in the temple on Mount Zion, later embodied in Messiah himself as the perfect heavenly temple (John 2:19-20), and ultimately transformed into a spiritual temple, comprised of his people, where God still dwells in their midst. In the Scriptures, the phrase "dwelling place for God" is used of the temple (Ezekiel 37:26; Acts 7:46-47).[9] The body of Christ on earth has become the spiritual Mount Zion, the heavenly Jerusalem, the final holy temple of God on earth:

> Hebrews 12:22, 24
> But you have come to Mount Zion and to the city of the living God, the heavenly Jerusalem, and to innumerable angels in festal gathering…and to Jesus, the mediator of a new covenant.

> Ephesians 2:19–22
> So then you are no longer strangers and aliens, but you are fellow citizens with the saints and members of the household of God [God's house = temple], built on the foundation of the apostles and prophets, Christ Jesus himself being the cornerstone, in whom the whole structure, being joined together, grows into a holy temple in the Lord. In him you

[8] W. Harold Mare, "Zion (Place)," in *The Anchor Yale Bible Dictionary*, ed. David Noel Freedman (New York: Doubleday, 1992), 1096.

[9] See also 1 Corinthians 3:16-17 and 2 Corinthians 6:16.

> also are being built together into a dwelling place for God by the Spirit.

But this beautiful and ultimate transformation of the mountain and temple is not easy. It is fraught with conflict. In Nebuchadnezzar's prophetic dream which Daniel interpreted, the kingdom of God that Messiah was to bring was described metaphorically as a rock uncut by human hands (i.e., Messiah) that hits a large metallic human image representing the Gentile kingdoms of history: "But the stone that struck the image became a great mountain and filled the whole earth" (Daniel 2:35). "And in the days of those [Gentile] kings the God of heaven will set up a kingdom that shall never be destroyed. … It shall break in pieces all these kingdoms and bring them to an end" (Daniel 2:44). Ever since Messiah came to earth during that dream's fourth kingdom, the ancient Roman empire, his kingdom mountain has been growing to fill the earth with ups and downs through much historic turmoil.

But God's Word is true. He will accomplish his purposes against those who reject him. This antagonistic portrayal of the kingdom of God as a mountain kingdom overthrowing other kingdoms is another biblical theme that plays out as the war of cosmic mountains.

Mount Hermon vs. Mount Zion

As we have already established in the Bible, the spiritual princes over nations and peoples reflect the conflict of earthly kingdoms and peoples. When there is a war on earth, there is a war in heaven. When powers on earth are overthrown, powers in heaven are shaken. In the *Judah Maccabee* novels, I depict this as the nations' conquering gods, known in the Bible as spiritual principalities and powers, overtaking cosmic mountains. When Greece overthrows Canaan, the Greek gods take over Mount Zaphon. When Rome beats Greece into submission, the Olympians lose their Mount Olympus. So, when the pagans overthrow and pollute with abomination the Jerusalem temple, then Yahweh leaves his house in judgment. It becomes desolate of his presence while inhabited by demons.

There is another cosmic mountain crucial to our developing narrative. Those familiar with all my Chronicles series novels will know Mount Hermon plays a significant role in the storyline because it plays a significant role in the Bible's theological storyline.

Let's start at the beginning. We have already established elsewhere that Genesis 6:1-4 describes divine beings, called Sons of God, coming down from heaven to mate with human women, resulting in hybrid offspring, called Nephilim.[10] These Nephilim and their counterparts—the Anakim, Rephaim, Emim, and other giant clans—are considered evil or demonic throughout the entire Bible. God considered the act of those angels "leaving their heavenly abode" to come to earth and seek after the "different flesh" of humans (Jude 6-7) sinful and punishable by imprisonment in Tartarus at the Genesis Flood (2 Peter 2:4).

But where exactly did these Sons of God come down? The Bible does not say specifically. But Intertestamental Jewish tradition argues for Mount Hermon as the locale of their nefarious activity. Mount Hermon is a part of the Anti-Lebanon mountain range in the northern territory that Joshua conquered (Joshua 11:17; 12:1). Hermon's peak is over nine thousand feet high and often covered with snow. It extends northeast to southwest about thirty miles of the ninety-three-mile-long mountain range. It has a reputation in the Bible for being a location of dark spiritual forces linked to Antediluvian times. But in order to understand that dark reputation's origin, let's begin with Second Temple literature that most explicitly introduces us to the tradition.

Though not Scripture, a particular manuscript of the book of 1 Enoch has been considered through most of Church history as a worthy source of religious reference. In fact, the New Testament book of Jude

---

[10] Brian Godawa, *When Giants Were Upon the Earth: The Watchers, the Nephilim, and the Biblical Cosmic War of the Seed*, (Los Angeles: Embedded Pictures Publishing, 2014).

quotes 1 Enoch in the context of the angelic sin we just mentioned (Jude 14-15).

Here is what 1 Enoch says about Mount Hermon and the Sons of God, also called "Watchers":

> 1 Enoch 6:1-6
> When the sons of men had multiplied, in those days, beautiful and comely daughters were born to them. And the watchers, the sons of heaven, saw them and desired them. And they said to one another, "Come, let us choose for ourselves wives from the daughters of men, and let us beget children for ourselves."
>
> And Shemihazah, their chief, said to them, "I fear that you will not want to do this deed, and I alone shall be guilty of a great sin."
>
> And they all answered him and said, "Let us all swear an oath, and let us all bind one another with a curse, that none of us turn back from this counsel until we fulfill it and do this deed."
>
> Then they all swore together and bound one another with a curse. And they were, all of them, two hundred, who descended in the days of Jared onto the peak of Mount Hermon. And they called the mountain "Hermon" because they swore and bound one another with a curse on it.[11]

There are several key elements of this passage from 1 Enoch that relate to our interest in cosmic mountains. First, the Genesis 6 sin of the angels/Watchers occurred in the "days of Jared." Genesis 11:15-18 tells us Jared was the father of Enoch, the famous holy man who "walked

[11] George W. E. Nickelsburg and James C. VanderKam, *1 Enoch: The Hermeneia Translation* (Minneapolis: Fortress Press, 2012), 23-24.

with God" and was translated to heaven just before the days of Noah. Luke 3:37 confirms Jared was Noah's great-grandfather. According to the unusually high longevities in the text's patriarchal genealogies, the Great Flood did not occur until almost one thousand years after this original incursion of the Sons of God from heaven on Mount Hermon.

Like all "holy mountains," the divine beings descended to the mountaintop, where they took an oath related to their dirty deed of taking human women as mates. They knew they were violating God's holy separation between earthly and heavenly beings, so they made sure they were all bound to stick with it, or they would be under a curse.

In 1869, British explorer Charles Warren discovered a sacred site atop Mount Hermon that contained a large oval pit five hundred yards in diameter, surrounded by a small stone wall that seems to have been used to guide ritualistic circumambulation of the pit. There is also a sacred temple that appears to be of later date outside the pit area.[12]

He also found a stone artifact engraved with the Greek words, "According to the command of the greatest and holy God, those who take an oath proceed from here."[13] While the stone's provenance was considered to be from the fourth century AD, the oval pit was considered much older. In my *Judah Maccabee* novels, I depict this sacred temple location along with the oath-stone as part of the supernatural storyline of the Watchers and cosmic mountains.

Enoch scholar George Nickelsburg makes the connection of that stone artifact with the Watchers' oath in 1 Enoch.[14] And the very name "Hermon" derives from the Hebrew HRM (*herem*),[15] which the Bible uses of idolatrous Canaanite giant clans, like the Anakim, who were

---

12 Charles Warren, R. E. [1840-1927], "The Summit of Hermon, With an Illustration," *Palestine Exploration Fund Quarterly Statement* 2.5 (Jan. 1 to March 31, 1870), 210-244.

13 Charles Simon Clermont-Ganneau, "Archaeological and Epigraphic Notes on Palestine," *Palestine Exploration Fund Quarterly Statement for 1903*, 35.2 (London: Palestine Exploration Fund, 1903), 135-140.

14 George W. E. Nickelsburg, *1 Enoch: A Commentary on the Book of 1 Enoch*, ed. Klaus Baltzer, *Hermeneia—a Critical and Historical Commentary on the Bible* (Minneapolis: Fortress, 2001), 247.

15 Rami Arav, "Hermon, Mount (Place)," in *The Anchor Yale Bible Dictionary*, ed. David Noel Freedman (New York: Doubleday, 1992), 158.

"devoted to destruction" (Joshua 11:21-22; Deuteronomy 20:17). Those *herem* peoples, it must be remembered, were linked to the offspring of the rebellious angelic Watchers and human women (Numbers 13:32-33).

But this spiritually occultic connection to Mount Hermon is not found only in Intertestamental literature; it is also in the Bible.

Before entering the Promised Land, Moses and Joshua defeated the kings of the Transjordan, one of whom was Og of Bashan, noted by Joshua as "one of the remnant of the Rephaim, who lived at Ashtaroth and at Edrei and ruled over Mount Hermon and Salecah and all Bashan" (Joshua 12:4–5).

We have already shown earlier in this book that the Rephaim were the cursed giants related to the original Nephilim offspring of the Watchers. But notice as well that Og ruled over Mount Hermon in the land of Bashan. Bashan in Hebrew means "place of the Serpent," ground zero for the Canaanite Cult of the Dead. As *The Dictionary of Deities and Demons* explains,

> For the 'Canaanites' of Ugarit, the Bashan region, or a part of it, clearly represented 'Hell', the celestial and infernal abode of their deified dead kings, Olympus and Hades at the same time. It is possible that this localization of the Canaanite Hell is linked to the ancient tradition of the place as the ancestral home of their dynasty, the *rpum* [Rephaim]. The Biblical text also recalls that "all Bashan used to be called the land/earth of the Rephaim" (Deut 3:13 [NEB]).[16]

So, the Bible shows us that Mount Hermon was the peak holy mountain in the land of the Rephaim, where the Canaanite Cult of the Dead worshipped the spirits of the demonic hybrid offspring of the Watchers and human women. Hermon was the cosmic mountain overshadowing

[16] del Olmo G. Lete, "Bashan," in *Dictionary of Deities and Demons in the Bible*, ed. Karel van der Toorn, Bob Becking, and Pieter W. van der Horst (Leiden; Boston; Köln; Grand Rapids, MI; Cambridge: Brill; Eerdmans, 1999), 162.

the land Moses and Joshua had to conquer and cleanse of its demonic infestation.

This context now brings clarity to a Davidic psalm that describes the Canaan's conquest as a contest between two cosmic mountains, Sinai and Hermon (described as "mountain of Bashan").

> Psalm 68:15–22
> O mountain of God, **mountain of Bashan [Mount Hermon**];
> O many-peaked mountain, **mountain of Bashan**!
> Why do you look with hatred, O many-peaked mountain,
> at the mount that God desired for his abode,
> yes, where the LORD will dwell forever?
> The chariots of God are twice ten thousand,
> thousands upon thousands;
> the Lord is among them; Sinai is now in the sanctuary.
> You ascended on high,
> leading a host of captives in your train
> and receiving gifts among men,
> even among the rebellious, that the LORD God may dwell there…
> But God will strike the heads of his enemies...
> The Lord said, "I will bring them back **from Bashan**,
> I will bring them back from the depths of the sea."

In this passage, David describes God coming from his holy mountain Sinai to take over Hermon, the mountain of Bashan, as his abode to dwell forever. A clash of cosmic mountains over the territory's ownership. God attacks that spiritual stronghold with his myriad of heavenly warriors on chariots.

But there is a New Covenant twist in this poem. When David writes, "You ascended on high leading a host of captives in your train," and bringing back his dead enemies "from the depths of the sea," he is not merely describing Joshua's conquest in the fifteenth century BC.

The inspired Apostle Paul links this same passage to Jesus Christ's resurrection and ascension in the New Covenant!

> Ephesians 4:8–11
> Therefore it says, "When he ascended on high he led a host of captives, and he gave gifts to men." (In saying, "He ascended," what does it mean but that he had also descended into the lower regions, the earth? He who descended is the one who also ascended far above all the heavens, that he might fill all things.)

Paul takes that cosmic mountain passage about Yahweh conquering Bashan and leading captives in a triumphal train of glory and applies it to Jesus as he led spiritual captives into heaven at his ascension. Paul then writes that the gifts Jesus/Yahweh gave to men were the gifts of the Holy Spirit to the Body of Christ, so as to equip them for service. And who were those captives but the spiritual principalities and powers over the nations he conquered through his death, resurrection and ascension (Colossians 2:15; Ephesians 6:12; 3:10)?[17]

But it is important to note that this was not merely Paul's appropriation of Intertestamental beliefs. Jesus himself alluded to the battle of cosmic mountains while with his disciples in Caesarea Philippi at the foot of none other than Mount Hermon. In Matthew 16, Jesus asked his disciples who they thought he was, and Peter famously declared, "You are the Christ, the Son of the living God!" (16:16), after which Jesus praised Peter's insight and announced,

> Matthew 16:18
> "And I tell you, you are Peter, and on this rock I will build my church, and the gates of hell [Hades] shall not prevail against it."

English translations get it wrong when they translate the word "Hades" as hell. In biblical theology, Hades is not hell. It is the place

[17] See also Ephesians 4:8-9; 2 Corinthians 2:14; Revelation 12:10-11; and 1 Peter 3:18-19.

where all the human dead go until their judgment, or until Messiah frees them. So Jesus was referring to the gates of Hades, the underworld, not the Lake of Fire at the end of time. Not even death would stop the onslaught of God's people advancing his kingdom. The perennial debate between Roman Catholics and Protestants has been whether the "rock" Jesus would build his Church upon was Peter or Peter's confessional statement.

Both viewpoints are wrong. We can prove this by looking at something too often overlooked: their location. Where are they? They are at Caesarea Philippi. This location had a long spiritual history rooted in the worship of the Greek satyr god Pan. In fact, there was a religious site called Panias (or Banias) just outside the city that is still there today. Scholar Judd Burton has explored this location as sacred geography and has found a connection of Pan to Azazel, one of the original Watchers who came down to Mount Hermon.[18] But more importantly, there is a cave at that site that contains a deep pit that the ancient Jewish historian Josephus said was believed to lead to the Abyss.[19] This was why this location was called the Gates of Hades.

You read that right. This sacred grotto was called by the same name that Jesus said his Church would overcome. Jesus and his disciples were almost certainly standing at Pan's grotto when he claimed his Church would be victorious. But was it just that little location to which he was referring? No. The Gates of Hades in Pan's grotto was located *at the foot of Mount Hermon*, already considered the cosmic mountain of Bashan, indeed of Canaan, whose history went back to the sin of the angels in Antediluvian days! The "rock" was neither Peter nor his confessional statement. The "rock" was the rocky mountain of Hermon that loomed above them. Jesus was claiming victory in the cosmic conflict of holy mountains that went back to the days of Moses

---

[18] Judd H. Burton, *Interview With the Giant: Ethnohistorical Notes on the Nephilim* (Burton Beyond Press, 2009) 19-21.

[19] *Wars of the Jews* 1:405, Flavius Josephus and William Whiston, The Works of Josephus: Complete and Unabridged (Peabody: Hendrickson, 1987).

described in Psalm 68. Mount Sinai vs. Mount Bashan became Mount Zion vs. Mount Bashan.

When Jesus defeated death through his own death and resurrection, he ascended to heaven to God's throne with the very keys to Hades. As Jesus said in Revelation 1:18, "I died, and behold I am alive forevermore, and I have the keys of Death and Hades." Mount Zion, the Church of Jesus Christ (Hebrews 12:22-24), has conquered Mount Hermon, the mountain of Bashan!

Chapter 7
Miscellaneous Oddities and Entities

The Foundation Stone

One of the interesting miscellaneous elements of research behind the *Judah Maccabee* novels is the Foundation Stone of the Jerusalem temple (in Hebrew, *Evan ha-Shetiyah*). In the novel, it rests in the Holy of Holies in the temple and covers a cave that accesses the Abyss, or the primeval waters of chaos, that lead to the underworld of Sheol (Hades in Greek).

This is not an entire fabrication by the author. It is rooted in real archaeology saturated in ancient Jewish legend. The Jerusalem temple's sacred Foundation Stone was a flat stone laid in the Holy of Holies upon which the Ark of the Covenant sat. There is even a depression in the existing stone that matches the ark's dimensions.[1]

Here is where it gets fascinating.

That Foundation Stone covers a small cave below the Holy of Holies that Muslims call "The Well of Souls" because they believed that they could hear within the restless spirits of the dead awaiting judgment.

The Bible links the Foundation Stone idea to the Messianic Cornerstone:

> Isaiah 28:16
> Therefore thus says the Lord GOD, "Behold, I am the one who has laid as a foundation in Zion, a stone, a tested

---

1 Been and Kathleen Ritmeyer, *Secrets of Jerusalem's Temple Mount* (Washington, DC: Biblical Archaeology Society, 1998), 104.

> stone, a precious cornerstone, of a sure foundation:
> 'Whoever believes will not be in haste.'

The Jews wrote a series of legends surrounding that stone in the Mishnah, Talmud, and other texts. One of them was that this was the rock upon which Abraham almost sacrificed his son Isaac.[2]

But even more foundational was their belief that the "construction of the earth was begun at the centre, with the foundation stone of the Temple, the Eben Shetiyah, for the Holy Land is at the central point of the surface of the earth."[3] Jerusalem was considered the navel of the earth and the Foundation Stone its very center, much like the Greeks considered their city of Delphi as the navel of the earth and the sacred Omphalos Stone in the temple of Delphi as the center of the earth.

More interestingly, the Talmud claims that the Foundation Stone was not only created as the center of the world but that the "pit of the altar…the cavity of the pits descended to the Abyss."[4] Ginzberg's *Legends of the Jews* relates another legend of the stone's origin when David was digging the temple's foundations deep within the earth. He found another rock, called a "shard," that spoke to him:

> David was about to lift it, when the shard exclaimed: 'Thou canst not do it.' 'Why not?' asked David. 'Because I rest upon the abyss.' 'Since when?' 'Since the hour in which the voice of God was heard to utter the words from Sinai, 'I am the Lord thy God,' causing the earth to quake and sink into the abyss. I lie here to cover up the abyss.' Nevertheless David lifted the shard, and the waters of the abyss rose and threatened to flood the earth…Thereupon Ahithophel [David's counsellor] had the Name of God

---

2 Pamela C. Berger, *The Crescent on the Temple: the Dome of the Rock as Image of the Ancient Jewish Sanctuary* (Boston: Brill), 24-25.

3 Ginzberg, Louis. *The Legends of the Jews — Volume 1* (p. 5). K-Edition.

4 (b. Yoma 5:2, II.1.A) Jacob Neusner, *The Babylonian Talmud: A Translation and Commentary,* vol. 5a (Peabody, MA: Hendrickson Publishers, 2011), 200. (b. Sukk. 4:9, V.3.A–4.B) Neusner, *The Babylonian Talmud,* 199.

> inscribed upon the shard, and the shard thrown into the abyss. The waters at once commenced to subside.[5]

So the Foundation Stone rests beneath the temple over the chaos waters of the Abyss, an important spiritual plot point in my *Judah Maccabee* novels. This entire Foundation Stone mythology comes to its conclusion as a spiritual phenomenon in my Chronicles of the Apocalypse series.

In that series I make a connection between the stone and Solomon's signet ring considered in Jewish legend to have binding power over demons. It was part of Solomon's reputation as an active exorcist.[6] Yet another legend says that Solomon received the signet ring from the archangel Michael with a "seal engraved on precious stone. …(with it) you [Solomon] shall imprison all the demons, both female and male, and with their help you shall build Jerusalem when you bear this seal of God."[7]

So, Solomon suppressed the dark spiritual forces in his building of the temple, as symbolically depicted in his seal upon the Foundation Stone over the Abyss. This is obviously not a biblical historical story, but it is a creative spiritual metaphor for the heavenly power of God's house in the earthly realm. The Jews believed that the Jerusalem temple on earth was linked to Yahweh's temple in heaven, and that mountains, like Mount Zion, were links between heaven, earth, and the underworld.[8]

---

[5] Ginzberg, Louis. *The Legends of the Jews — Volume 4* (K Locations 958-966). K-Edition.

[6] Flavius Josephus and William Whiston, *The Works of Josephus: Complete and Unabridged* (Peabody, MA: Hendrickson, 1987) Antiquities 8.42-47. See also Wisdom of Solomon 7:15–22 and the Testament of Solomon (entire book), James H. Charlesworth, *The Old Testament Pseudepigrapha, vol. 1* (New York; London: Yale University Press, 1983), 960-987.

[7] Testament of Solomon 1:6-7. James H. Charlesworth, *The Old Testament Pseudepigrapha*, vol. 1 (New York; London: Yale University Press, 1983), 962.

[8] See my section on "Cosmic Mountains" in Brian Godawa, *When Watchers Ruled the Nations: Pagan Gods at War with Israel's God and the Spiritual World of the Bible* (Allen, TX: Warrior Poet Publishing, 2021), 327-333.

Amulets and Charms

There is a small artifact that I use in the story of Judah Maccabee that reflects a fascinating and confirmed archeological fact. I refer to an amulet with a blessing that Hannah, Judah's mother, gives to his pregnant wife, Sophia.

In my book *The Spiritual World of Jezebel and Elijah*, I describe the archaeological evidence for pagan family shrines and magical amulets and charms in ancient Israel around 800 BC. This evidence reflected the folk religion of many rural and city Jews, as well as some in the Jewish priesthood, in contrast with the prophets who sought Yahweh's holiness in Israel.[9]

It was common for Hebrews to assimilate aspects of their captor's culture, such as adopting some of their pagan superstitions. This was precisely part of the cause of Israel's "unfaithfulness" to Yahweh that brought on the Exile hundreds of years later.

Judean tombs of these periods have included items used for divination and "magic," including dice, and sheep/goat knuckles used for casting lots, amulets, and other good luck charms considered "apotropaic" devices used to ward off evil. "Among the most conspicuous apotropaic devices in late Judean tombs are Egyptian-style glazed Bes figurines and Eye-of-Horus amulets, whose function as popular good-luck charms throughout the Levant is well known."[10]

The Eye of Horus was an Egyptian symbol of protection and health. Bes was an ugly Egyptian dwarf deity with a lion's face, bowed legs, and sometimes depicted with an enormous phallus.[11] Though Bes was not worshipped per se, his image is found on Israelite vessels, household

---

[9] Brian Godawa, *The Spiritual World of Jezebel and Elijah: Biblical Background to the Novel Jezebel: Harlot Queen of Israel* (Allen, TX: Warrior Poet Publishing, 2021), 106-112.

[10] William G. Dever, *The Lives of Ordinary People in Ancient Israel: Where Archaeology and the Bible Intersect* (Grand Rapids, MI; Cambridge: William B. Eerdmans Publishing Company, 2012), 271–273.

[11] H. te Velde, "Bes," ed. Karel van der Toorn, Bob Becking, and Pieter W. van der Horst, *Dictionary of Deities and Demons in the Bible* (Leiden; Boston; Köln; Grand Rapids, MI; Cambridge: Brill; Eerdmans, 1999), 173.

items, and amulets for the protection of children and pregnant mothers in their childbirth.[12]

More recent discoveries have brought to light Jewish amulets of both blessing and cursing that go back to the days of Moses. A curse amulet was found at, predictably, Mount Ebal, where the Bible says was a place of curse (Deuteronomy 27:9-26). It is a small one-inch piece of lead folded in half that contains the words, "You are cursed by the god yhw, cursed. You will die, cursed—cursed, you will surely die. Cursed you are by yhw—cursed."[13]

An example of amulets of blessing dated to around the seventh century BC was found near Jerusalem in 1979. They were tiny silver scrolls rolled up to be worn as jewelry, carrying the biblical blessing from Numbers 6:24-26: "May YHWH bless you and guard you; may YHWH make his face shine upon you."[14]

The Jewish Virtual Library (JVL) explains the purpose of these amulets:

> In pre-modern days, the female was viewed as weak and in need of protection. The custom was developed for people to have pieces of paper, parchment, or metal discs inscribed with various formulae that would protect the bearer from sickness, the "evil eye," and other troubles. The use of inscription as a means to ward off evil spirits stemmed from a belief in early times in the holiness and in the power of words.[15]

But was this practice of pagan word protection continued from the early years of Moses into the second century BC? Actually, yes. Jews continued it up to the Medieval period and into present-day Middle

[12] "Found in Jerusalem's City of David: The Egyptian God Bes": https://www.haaretz.com/archaeology/MAGAZINE-found-in-jerusalem-s-city-of-david-egyptian-god-bes-1.7042407

[13] Nathan Steinmeyer "An Early Israelite Curse Inscription from Mt. Ebal?" *Biblical Archaeology Society* website May 19, 2023. https://www.biblicalarchaeology.org/daily/biblical-artifacts/inscriptions/mt_ebal_inscription/

[14] Prof.Shawna Dolansky, "Birkat Kohanim: The Magic of a Blessing," *The Torah* website https://www.thetorah.com/article/birkat-kohanim-the-magic-of-a-blessing

[15] "Amulet," Jewish Virtual Library website, https://www.jewishvirtuallibrary.org/amulet

Eastern practices. And the JVL explains that Talmud frequently uses a word that means "to bind," indicating its purpose of binding evil spirits, the evil eye, sicknesses, or curses.

One of the protective amulets' ongoing purposes was for childbirth. As the JVL explains, "a compilation of magic, cosmology, and mystical teachings popular among both Ashkenazi and Sephardi communities, contained a recipe for an inscribed amulet to protect a laboring woman as well as for an amulet for a newborn specifically directed against Lilith."[16]

Lilith had an ancient Mesopotamian mythology that Jews adapted into their own. Lilith was known as the demon who stole away newborn babies to suck their blood, eat their bone marrow, and consume their flesh.[17] In Jewish legends, she was described as having long hair and wings, and claimed to have been Adam's first wife, who was banished because of Adam's unwillingness to accept her as his equal.[18]

Lilith appears in the Bible along with other pagan mythical creatures, like the satyr, a demonized interpretation of the goat-like god Pan. Her name is poorly translated into English as "the night hag." In Isaiah 34, prophetic judgment upon Edom involves its transformation into a desert wasteland inhabited by all kinds of demonic creatures: ravens, jackals, hyenas, satyrs, and—Lilith.

> Isaiah 34:13–15 (RSV)
> It shall be the haunt of jackals... And wild beasts [*siyyim*] shall meet with hyenas [*iyyim*], the satyr shall cry to his fellow; yea, there shall the night hag [*Lilith*] alight, and find for herself a resting place.

---

[16] "Amulet," Jewish Virtual Library website, https://www.jewishvirtuallibrary.org/amulet

[17] Handy, Lowell K. "Lilith (Deity)", in *The Anchor Yale Bible Dictionary*, ed. David Noel Freedman (New York: Doubleday, 1992), 324-325.

[18] Ginzberg, Louis; Szold, Henrietta (2011-01-13). *Legends of the Jews*, all four volumes in a single file, improved 1/13/2011 (Kindle Locations 1016-1028). B&R Samizdat Express. Kindle Edition.

The Hebrew words for "wild beasts" and "hyenas" (*iyyim*) are not readily identifiable,[19] so the ESV translators simply guessed according to their anti-mythical bias and filled in their translations with naturalistic words like "wild beasts" and "hyenas." But of these words, Bible commentator Hans Wildberger says,

> The creatures that are mentioned in v. 14 cannot be identified zoologically, not because we are not provided with enough information, but because they refer to fairy tale and mythical beings. *Siyyim* are demons, the kind that do their mischief by the ruins of Babylon, according to [Isaiah] 13:21. They are mentioned along with the *iyyim* (goblins) in this passage.[20]

The Dictionary of Biblical Languages (DBL) admits that another interpretation of *iyyim*, other than howling desert animals, is "spirit, ghost, goblin, i.e., a night demon or dead spirit (Isa. 13:22; 34:14; Jer. 50:39), note: this would be one from the distant lands, i.e., referring to the nether worlds."[21]

One could say that *siyyim and iyyim* are similar to our own homophonic play on words, "ghosts and goblins." And Isaiah's prophecy is the equivalent of saying that demons will dance on your graves.[22]

Drawing Down the Moon

The pagan ritual phrase "drawing down the moon" is well known in modern-day paganism and Wicca religion (modern witchcraft). It involves the high priestess of a coven of witches engaging in rituals beneath a lunar sky wherein she enters a trance and calls upon "the

---

[19] "Siyyim," Francis Brown, Samuel Rolles Driver, and Charles Augustus Briggs, *Enhanced Brown-Driver-Briggs Hebrew and English Lexicon* (Oak Harbor, WA: Logos Research Systems, 2000), 850.

[20] Hans Wildberger, *A Continental Commentary: Isaiah 28–39* (Minneapolis: Fortress Press, 2002).

[21] James Swanson, *Dictionary of Biblical Languages With Semantic Domains: Hebrew (Old Testament)*, electronic ed. (Oak Harbor, WA: Logos Research Systems, Inc., 1997).

[22] The demons and goblins (*siyyim* and *iyyim*) also appear in Isaiah 13:21-22 and Jeremiah 50:39.

Goddess" to enter the priestess in a kind of all-encompassing, divine embodiment of the feminine.

But what would surprise some readers is that this occult ritual has an ancient history that goes back to Greek witchcraft rooted in erotic magic. The ancient Greek city of Thessaly was notorious for witches engaging in the erotic drawing-down-the-moon ritual to such an extent that they referred to it as "the Thessalian crime."[23] The poet Menander wrote a play titled *Thessalian Women* that sought to expose the deceits of this ritual.

A now-lost ancient Greek vase art from about the second century BC illustrates two naked Thessalian witches engaged in the ritual that was usually performed with the purpose of erotic attraction magic.

Professor of ancient history Daniel Ogden draws from ancient sources to list some aspects of the ritual as being the use of incantations, a special spinning "rhombus" wheel, the clashing of bronze cymbals, and the digging of a pit, which was believed to turn the moon blood red and even have some control of the moon, sun, and stars as well as time itself.[24]

The *Judah Maccabee* novels include a scene of Greek goddesses engaging in a drawing-down-the-moon ritual adapted to achieve sexual unity with the dead World Tree called Gaia. Their purpose: to resurrect Gaia with the spirit of the Goddess.

---

[23] Daniel Ogden, *Magic, Witchcraft, and Ghosts in the Greek and Roman Worlds: A Source Book* (New York: Oxford University Press, 2002), 236.

[24] Ogden, *Magic, Witchcraft*, 236-240, 254.

APPENDIX
The Future Abomination of Desolation in Daniel 9 and 12

(Adapted from the Appendix in
Judah Maccabee: Part 2 – Against the Gods of Greece)

Daniel 9:26–27
And the people of the prince who is to come shall destroy the city and the sanctuary. Its end shall come with a flood, and to the end there shall be war. **Desolations** are decreed. And he shall make a strong covenant with many for one week, and for half of the week he shall put an end to sacrifice and offering. And on **the wing of abominations shall come one who makes desolate,** until the decreed end is poured out on the **desolate**."

Daniel 12:11
And from the time that the regular burnt offering is taken away and the **abomination that makes desolate** is set up, there shall be 1,290 days.

Spoken of by Daniel

As we saw earlier, Antiochus IV Epiphanes fulfilled the prophecies about the abomination of desolation in Daniel chapters 8 and 11. But there are two other passages in Daniel that talk about a second abomination of desolation to come long after Antiochus Epiphanes is gone. This abomination appears as indicated above in chapters 9 and 12. This is not partial or dual fulfillment but a biblically defined second abomination of desolation that is different from the first.

I do not have the space here to explore this topic exhaustively. It is one of those prophecies that has a dozen different interpretations. I recommend *The Seventy Weeks and the Great Tribulation* by Philip Mauro. Some Bible scholars suggest that the abomination of desolation spoken of in Daniel 9 and 12 is the same being as in Daniel 8 and 11. But they cannot be the same for three big reasons I have previously stated. One, the first abomination by Antiochus was described as only a desecration of the temple (religious pollution) while the second abomination includes both the desolation *and* the destruction of that temple, as well as the city (9:26). That is a very big difference. Two, the period of desolation for the first abomination was 2,300 days, or evenings and mornings (Daniel 8:14), while the period of desolation for the second abomination would be 1,290 days (Daniel 12:11). Three, the first abomination was to occur long *before* "the time of the end" (Daniel 11:27, 35) while the second abomination was explicitly stated to occur *during* "the time of the end" (Daniel 11:40; 12:4, 9), at "the end of days" (Daniel 12:13). No matter how one interprets "the end," it is a definite time period that was to occur long after that first abomination of desolation.

The informed reader will naturally ask if this is the abomination that Jesus predicted.

> Matthew 24:15–20
> [Jesus:] "So when you see the **abomination of desolation** spoken of by the prophet Daniel, standing in the holy place (let the reader understand)

I believe it is. And I will address Jesus later. For now, I want to see where Daniel himself is pointing. Then we will look at how Jesus confirms that future monster.

So, who is this second abominable desolator to come? Let's take a closer look at Daniel 9.

The Seventy Weeks

Probably the most famous messianic prophecy in the Old Testament is Daniel's vision of the 70 Weeks. This is because it predicts the coming Messiah within a specific number of years from a specific historical event—the decree to restore and rebuild Jerusalem, most likely fulfilled in the decree of Artaxerxes I around 457 BC (Nehemiah 2:1). From 457 BC to AD 30 (the death of Jesus the Anointed One) is 487 years, the middle of the 70th week of years (Daniel 9:27).[1]

The English phrase "70 weeks" is a translation of the Hebrew "70 sevens" of years, or 490 years. That chronology would place Messiah in the very lifetime of Jesus.[2] This is why messianic expectation was so high in the first century. But it also places the arrival of Messiah right before the arrival of one who would set up an "abomination of desolation," going on to defile and destroy both Jerusalem and her holy temple. Just exactly how are these two things, the Anointed One and Abomination, related in time and space? And what do they have to do with the abomination of desolation in the days of the Maccabees as discussed earlier in this book? Let's take a closer look at the 70 Weeks prophecy.

> Daniel 9:24–27
> 24 Seventy weeks are decreed about your people and your
> holy city, to finish the transgression, to put an end to sin,
> and to atone for iniquity, to bring in everlasting
> righteousness, to seal both vision and prophet, and to
> anoint the most holy. 25 Know therefore and understand
> that from the going out of the word to restore and build
> Jerusalem to the coming of an anointed one, a prince, there
> shall be seven weeks. Then for sixty-two weeks it shall be

---

[1] It is important to note that our dates for these events are not set in stone. At best, we can only get close, but not exact, as much as some Christians would prefer. Jay Rogers, *The Prophecy of Daniel in Preterist Perspective: The Easy Parts and the Hard Parts* (Media House, 2021), 13.

[2] Another theory is that the decree to restore and rebuild Jerusalem was that of Cyrus the Great of Babylon in 538 BC, which would still place Messiah in the rough time period of Jesus. In this view, the prophecy does not claim scientific precision, but rather approximation, which is not unwarranted in prophetic interpretation.

> built again with squares and moat, but in a troubled time. [26] And after the sixty-two weeks, an anointed one shall be cut off and shall have nothing. And the people of the prince who is to come shall destroy the city and the sanctuary. Its end shall come with a flood, and to the end there shall be war. Desolations are decreed. [27] And he shall make a strong covenant with many for one week, and for half of the week he shall put an end to sacrifice and offering. And on the wing of abominations shall come one who makes desolate, until the decreed end is poured out on the desolate.

Let's take a closer look at the first part of this passage. Daniel's prophecy was given to Israel. Because Israel had been unfaithful to Yahweh, he had punished his people with exile in Babylon, the city from which Daniel was writing. When Daniel states that 70 weeks is decreed for God's holy people and city, he is referring to Jeremiah's prophecy that the exile would last for 70 years (Jeremiah 25:8-12). Daniel is now amplifying that the 70 years of judgment would be multiplied because of the multiplied wickedness of Israel (Daniel 9:2, 5-7). Though they would come back from exile in 70 years as promised (Ezra 1:1), their transgression would not be forgiven for 70 weeks of years. The Hebrew word for "weeks" is actually seven. So Daniel is saying that the prophecy will be fulfilled within 70 sevens of years, or 490 years. At the end of that time, the Anointed One, Messiah, would arrive to complete the punishment and bring in the New Covenant of forgiveness.

When Daniel wrote of "**finishing the transgression, to put an end to sin and atone for iniquity**" (9:24), he was writing about the sin of Israel. When Messiah came, he would put an end to sin and atone for Israel's transgression of continuing disobedience to Yahweh. This was fulfilled when the angel of the Lord told Mary to call her child Jesus, "for he will save his people from their sins" (Matthew 1:21). When Jesus cried out "It is finished" on the cross, he was putting an end to sin with his once-for-all sacrifice that atoned for iniquity and **brought in everlasting righteousness**, just as Daniel prophesied (Hebrews 9:12-14).

Jesus confirmed the promise, or "**sealed both vision and prophet**" (Daniel 9:24), in fulfilling the messianic promise to which all the prophets had looked forward (1 Peter 1:10-12). Jesus was the seal on the scroll of God's prophecies. And he was the "**anointed, most holy**." The English translation that there was to be an "anointing of a most holy *place*" is not in the original language. In the Hebrew, it only says "anoint a most holy." Contextually, that would be Jesus. Since Jesus was the Anointed One, he was the most holy for only he could stand in the Holy of Holies of Yahweh's temple as our perfect sinless high priest.

The prophecy then returns to proclaim when this prophecy clock would begin. But this is sometimes translated in a confusing way that throws off interpretations. Does Messiah the prince come after the first seven weeks as the ESV translates or after 69 weeks (7+62)? The NASB95 cuts through that confusion with some clarity.

> Daniel 9:25 (NASB95)
> "So you are to know and discern *that* from the issuing of a decree to restore and rebuild Jerusalem until Messiah the Prince *there will be* seven weeks and sixty-two weeks; it will be built again, with plaza and moat, even in times of distress.

Consider reading the passage this way. There are three events coming—the decree about Jerusalem, its actual rebuilding, and the coming of Messiah. Those are three events within two different time periods. The first event, the decree, launches the first time period of 7 sevens, or 49 years. The city of Jerusalem was rebuilt in Nehemiah's day within 49 years after the decree during the "**times of distress**" or "**troubled times**" of Nehemiah 4:18. Then after the next 62 sevens of years, or about 483 years after the decree, the prophecy predicted the coming of Messiah. Messiah comes after 7+62 weeks of years, or 483 years.

After Messiah comes (i.e., after that 62nd week), he would be "**cut off and shall have nothing**" (Daniel 9:26). We see this fulfilled in Jesus's words on the cross: "My God, my God, why have you forsaken me?" (Matthew 27:46, taken from Psalm 22:1). Sin cuts off spiritual relationship. "For our sake he made [Jesus] to be sin who knew no sin, so that in him we might become the righteousness of God" (2 Corinthians 5:21).

Messianic Context of Daniel 9:24-26	
Daniel Verse	**New Testament Fulfillment**
Finish the transgression.	Daniel 9:5-6, 10-11.
Put an end to sin.	Hebrews 9:26; 1:3.
Atone for iniquity.	Colossians 1:14; John 1:29; 1 John 2:2.
Bring in everlasting righteousness.	2 Corinthians 9:9; Daniel 7:14; Matthew 6:33; 1 Corinthians 1:30.
Seal both vision and prophet.	Luke 18:31; 24:44; 21:22; Matthew 5:17-18.
Anoint a most holy place.	Luke 4:17–21; Isaiah 61:1-2.
Temple rebuilt in troubled times.	Nehemiah 4:18.
Messiah cut off and have nothing.	Matthew 27:46 (Psalm 22:1); 2 Corinthians 5:21.

So, 69 of the 70 weeks are fulfilled up to the time of Messiah Jesus. But the text actually says that the Messiah is cut off "after" 69 weeks (7 + 62). So, his cutting off occurs sometime after his arrival at the start of the 70th week. Jesus started his ministry at age 30 around the years AD 27-29. That was the end of the 69th week and the beginning of the 70th week. And we know that about 3-1/2 years into his ministry, Jesus was crucified. Remember that 3-1/2 years because it is going to be important.

Next, we are told that a people of the "**prince to come**" shall destroy the city and sanctuary (Jerusalem and the temple). Some link this prince to the one who later "comes on the wing of abominations" (Daniel 9:27). I do not believe this to be the case because in the previous verse, the Messiah ("anointed one") is described as *the prince who is to* *come*. There are not two princes here. There is only one, and he is the Messiah prince.

Christians might react negatively to this by asking how it is possible that the Messiah would destroy Jerusalem and the temple. After all, it was the Romans who destroyed Jerusalem and the temple in AD 70. Therefore, they must be the people of the "prince to come" this passage is talking about. To many Bible readers, it may sound contradictory to call the invading Roman armies "the people of Messiah." But biblically speaking, this is exactly how God talks. Whenever God judges a city or a people, he sovereignly uses pagan armies to achieve his purposes, and he describes the event as God's own armies or servants bringing judgment. Indeed, the pagan armies are often described as God's own hand bringing judgment. They are in effect, God's people or instruments.[3]

When Israel first entered the Promised Land, Yahweh told them that if they would disobey him, he would "bring a [foreign] nation against you from far away, from the end of the earth, swooping down like the eagle" (Deuteronomy 28:49).

When God judged Israel in Isaiah's day, God stated that he was using the pagan nation of Assyria and her king as an axe in his own hand (Isaiah 10:5, 15-16), that it was God who sent the Assyrians against Israel (v 6).

When the first temple and Jerusalem were destroyed by the Babylonians in 586 BC, Yahweh described Nebuchadnezzar as "his servant" and the invading pagan armies as his tribes sent upon Israel (Jeremiah 25:8-9).

When Babylon was then overthrown by the Medes, Isaiah described it as Yahweh mustering and sending his own army host (the pagan Medes) to punish and make the land a desolation (Isaiah 13:1-5, 11).

---

[3] Interestingly, even if one interprets this "prince to come" as a king separate from Messiah whose people destroy the sanctuary and city, it still fits with my paradigm. For I will argue that the "prince" or king was Titus Vespasian, Roman Imperial ruler of the Roman armies.

So it is most consistent with Scripture to understand that Daniel is saying that the Messiah will be the one who destroys Jerusalem and her temple by sending a pagan army to do his work of judgment.

And that destruction of Jerusalem would happen *after* Messiah was cut off.

We know Jesus was cut off from the Father on the cross sometime around AD 29-32. So how long after the cross is the destruction of Jerusalem and the temple? Some Christian prophecy pundits impose a two-thousand-year gap here and say that the last seven years of the prophecy have been put on hold to be fulfilled in our future. This prince must be a future "Antichrist" who destroys a new temple that has been rebuilt after its destruction in AD 70.

This is problematic for a couple reasons. First, there is no reference in the text to a *second* rebuilt temple, only to the temple that was built after 49 years in the days of Nehemiah. The text says that this rebuilt temple will be destroyed *after* Messiah is cut off. Historically, this occurred a mere generation after Jesus Christ was cut off from the Father on the cross. There is only one destruction and one rebuilt temple in the text. So when futurists insert a belief in a *second* rebuilt temple and *second* destruction after the one that actually happened in history, they are adding to the Word of God, not exegeting it.

Do you see the pattern of adding gaps where there are none in the text and skipping over biblically significant events for imaginary ones? In Daniel 2, they skip over the prophecy of Christ's first coming and apply it to the second coming. Now, they skip over the actual prophesied destruction of the temple and apply it to a future destruction of a temple that the text never claims will be built.

There is also no indication in Daniel's prophecy of a time gap between any of the weeks of years as some futurists seek to impose. These prophecy speculators believe that everything in the first 69 or 69-1/2 weeks of years was fulfilled by the time period of Messiah Jesus. But depending on their interpretation, they believe that either the last 7 years of the prophecy or the last 3-1/2 years of the prophecy have yet to be fulfilled in our current future. They place a gap of over two thousand years into the prophecy to maintain it is not yet entirely fulfilled, therefore we are still waiting for the last 7 or last 3-1/2 years to happen.

The big problem with this gap theory is that the seventy sevens of years are described as occurring continuously *without a gap*. There is not even the slightest hint of a gap of thousands of years between any of the continuous 70 weeks of years. Inserting a gap of two thousand years reveals a preconceived system that imposes an external artificial construct which does not exist in the actual biblical text.

So what did happen to that last 7-year part of the prophecy after Messiah? The answer can be found in the very next verse. In Daniel 9:27, we read that "***he* shall make a covenant with many for one week, and for half of the week, he shall put an end to sacrifice and offering.**" Many futurists interpret this "he" to be a so-called Antichrist and that the last week of years is a seven-year tribulation in the distant future. In their speculative paradigm, this Antichrist supposedly makes a treaty with Israel that he breaks after three-and-a-half years. Then he puts an end to sacrifices in a rebuilt temple in Jerusalem.

But the grammar of the Daniel text does not support this interpretation. In fact, the "he" referred to in verse 27 is grammatically a reference to the prior **Messiah prince**. "He," the prince in this passage who makes a covenant and puts an end to sacrifice, is the Christ, NOT the Antichrist. It is literally the opposite of what many prophecy speculators suggest. As scholar Kenneth Gentry has written:

> The indefinite pronoun "he" … refers back to the last dominant individual mentioned: "Messiah" (v. 26a). The Messiah is the leading figure in the whole prophecy, so that even the destruction of the Temple is related to His death.

> In fact, the people who destroy the Temple are providentially "His armies" (Matthew 22:2-7).[4]

Let's reread the prophecy and that seventieth week with this clarity.

> Daniel 9:27
> And he [Messiah] shall make a strong [new] covenant with many [remnant believers] for one week, and for half of the week he [Messiah] shall put an end to sacrifice and offering [the cross ends sacrifice and offering].

So we see that the initiation of the new covenant kingdom begins with Christ's ministry (Matthew 4:17). The "half-week" of years is not in the middle of some 7-year tribulation future to us. It represents the approximate 3-1/2 years of Christ's ministry. Jesus was crucified and therefore cut off from the Father 3-1/2 years into that 70th week of years. That is the creation of the new covenant.

In the Bible, Satan does not make covenants with God's people. God does. The "strong covenant" cannot therefore be of an Antichrist. It is the new covenant of the Christ. The earlier verse in Daniel 9 already stated it was Messiah who would "**put an end to sin and atone for iniquity**" (9:24), not some future Antichrist. It was Jesus Christ's sacrifice that put an end to sacrifices and offerings once and for all (Hebrews 10:12).

It is also important to note that while the abomination of desolation in both the past and future versions in Daniel "takes away the daily burnt offering" (Daniel 11:31, 12:11), the text says that what Messiah the Prince does is different. With his once-for-all sacrifice on the cross, Messiah "puts an end to sin and atones for iniquity" (Daniel 9:24) and "puts an end to sacrifice and offering" (Daniel 9:27). The Abomination forcibly defies the covenant. The Anointed One fulfills and brings the covenant to an end.

---

4 Dr. Kenneth L. Gentry, Jr., "Daniel's Seventy Weeks," (Covenant Media Foundation). http://www.cmfnow.com/articles/pt551.htm

So if Jesus put an end to sacrifice at the cross 3-1/2 years into the final 70th week of prophecy, what happens in the last 3-1/2 years of that last week of years? Nothing needs to happen. The break in the middle of the last week is a prophetic sign of the brokenness of Messiah at that point. That perfect last seven is broken in the middle by the cross. But because of that break in the 70th week, within the next three and a half years, the gospel was spreading all over the world to the Gentiles.

Now for the last verse of the passage. This is where the abomination is finally noted. And this is finally a different individual than the Messiah prince. This one is called "the one who makes desolate."

> Daniel 9:27
> And on the wing of **abominations** shall come **one who makes desolate**, until the decreed end is poured out on the **desolate**.

As we noted earlier, this is not the exact term "abomination of desolation," but it is a confluence of those exact terms in synonymous parallel. And this desolation is tied back to the previous verse 26 that describes the destruction of the city and sanctuary. "Its end shall come with flood, and to the end there shall be war. Desolations are decreed." Can you see how the two things are connected? Messiah ends old covenant sacrifice with the cross, then the city and temple of old covenant sacrifices are destroyed by an abominable one shortly afterward. In fact, within a generation.

So who is this abominable "one who makes desolate"?

Titus Vespasian

I will argue that the Roman general Titus Caesar Vespasianus is the bringer of the second abomination of desolation spoken of in Daniel 9 and 12. This occurred at the city of Jerusalem in the time period of AD 66-70. Let me set the historical stage for this fulfillment. In his Olivet discourse of Matthew 24, Jesus prophesied the destruction of the temple in Jerusalem of his day as God's judgment for their rejection of Messiah.

> Matthew 23:37-24:2
> "O Jerusalem, Jerusalem, the city that kills the prophets and stones those who are sent to it! How often would I have gathered your children together as a hen gathers her brood under her wings, and you were not willing! See, your house [holy temple] is left to you desolate...."
> Jesus left the temple and was going away, when his disciples came to point out to him the buildings of the temple. But he answered them, "You see all these, do you not? Truly, I say to you, there will not be left here one stone upon another that will not be thrown down."

Within 40 years of Jesus's prediction, the temple was destroyed just as he had predicted. This resulted from a Jewish revolt in Judea, then a province of Roman rule, around AD 66. The political, religious, and historical details of this series of events has fortunately been left to us in the writings of a Jewish historian named Flavius Josephus. His book *The Wars of the Jews* chronicles the narrative from before the revolt in AD 66 all the way up to the final destruction of the city of Jerusalem and its temple in AD 70.

At the time of the Jewish revolt, Nero was still Caesar of Rome, and he had been persecuting the Christians. This was the wicked king under whose reign the apostles like Peter and Paul were martyred. It was a major spiritual turning point in history for both Judaism and Christianity. In AD 67, Nero had sent his general Vespasian to quench the Jewish revolt. But when Nero died in 68, Vespasian came back to Rome to become the next Caesar. He sent his son Titus to finish the job in his stead.

Titus was a competent military general, but the revolt was widespread and took 3-1/2 years to put down (does that 3-1/2 number sound prophetically familiar?). He was described by Roman historian

Suetonius as "the darling of the human race," a "highly educated Roman noble with diplomatic skill that served to conceal both his efficiency and his ruthlessness."[5] As a family representative of Vespasian, Titus was considered to carry the authority of Caesar. He was even called Caesar during the war.[6]

Titus first swept through Judea, subduing most of the Jewish cities before ending up in AD 69 at Jerusalem, where he besieged the city for 5 months before conquering it and entering the holy city and temple.

A story of Titus from the Talmud illustrates his blasphemous, abominable nature. It is written that Titus had entered the temple, now empty of its treasures, and demanded, "Where is their God, the rock in whom they trusted?" He then "blasphemed and raged against Heaven.... He took a whore by her hand, and went into the house of the Holy of Holies; he spread out a scroll of the Torah, and on it he f****d her."[7]

Josephus explains that the Romans brought their standards into the temple, "and there did they offer sacrifices to them, and there did they make Titus imperator, with the greatest acclamations of joy."[8] Roman standards included an image of Caesar as god. They were a pagan abomination that signaled God's desolating absence from the temple.[9]

Josephus then claims that Titus plundered the temple of its treasures and ordered all the surviving priests to be put to death to perish along with the temple.[10] According to Josephus, the temple was burnt on the same exact day, the 10th day of the month Ab, "upon which [the first temple] was formerly burnt by the king of Babylon."

---

[5] Brian W. Jones, "Titus (Emperor)," ed. David Noel Freedman, *The Anchor Yale Bible Dictionary* (New York: Doubleday, 1992), 581.

[6] Dio Cassius, *Histories* 65.1.1-4: "Vespasian was declared emperor by the senate also, and Titus and Domitian were given the title of Caesars. The consular office was assumed by Vespasian and Titus while the former was in Egypt and the latter in Palestine."

[7] *Babylonian Talmud Gittin* 5:6, I.12.A–D. Jacob Neusner, *The Babylonian Talmud: A Translation and Commentary, vol. 11b* (Peabody, MA: Hendrickson Publishers, 2011), 243–244.

[8] Flavius Josephus, *The Wars of the Jews* 6.6.1, §316.

[9] Flavius Josephus, *The Wars of the Jews* 2.9.2 §169-170.

[10] Flavius Josephus, *The Wars of the Jews* 6.6.1, §316, 321

The historian concludes that in the Roman war with the Jews, 1,100,00 Jews perished and 97,000 were taken into slavery. He concludes with hyperbolic words that echo Jesus: "Accordingly the multitude of those that therein perished exceeded all the destructions that either men or God ever brought upon the world."[11]

Of this city and sanctuary destruction, Daniel 9:26 says, "Its end shall come with a flood, and to the end there shall be war." The use of "flood" here is not a literal tsunami of water but a metaphoric description of the overwhelming speed and unstoppable force of God's judgment, a common image in Old Testament prophecy (Isaiah 28:17; Jeremiah 47:2). But there's even more to it than that. The use of flood language evokes Noah's flood, which was theologically communicated in Genesis as being a symbolic return to the chaos of pre-creation in order for God to start over with the creation of a new covenant with Noah. Biblically speaking, the destruction of the Jerusalem temple was symbolic of God reducing the old covenant system as embodied in that temple into chaos so he could establish his "new creation," the new covenant through Christ (2 Corinthians 5:17).[12]

So Titus would perfectly fit Daniel's prophetic portrayal of the "one who comes on the wing of abominations and makes desolate" by destroying both city and temple and bringing abomination and desolation to that sacred space. What's more, the desolation/destruction took place after Messiah made his new covenant just 40 years earlier—just as Daniel's prophecy stated. The Jerusalem temple was the incarnation of the old covenant. So once the new covenant was established, the old covenant symbol, the temple, was destroyed by God through the abominable pagan leader Titus (Hebrews 8:13; 9:8-9).

---

[11] Flavius Josephus, *The Wars of the Jews* 6.9.3-4, §420, 429.

[12] For more detail on the temple and the New Covenant, see, Brian Godawa, Israel in Bible Prophecy: The New Testament Fulfillment of the Promise to Abraham (Warrior Poet Publishing, 2021), 47-53. Interestingly, the first temple being destroyed by the Babylonians in 586 BC was also described by the prophets Isaiah and Jeremiah as a decreation return to chaos: Isaiah 24:1-23; Jeremiah 4:23-26.

But we are not done with the abomination of desolation. There is one last passage in Daniel 12:11 that mentions it again. And again, the entire chapter has often been interpreted as yet-to-take-place in our future. And yet again, I would argue for a first century fulfillment of the second abomination of desolation under the actions of Titus Vespasian, the "one who makes desolate."

Let's run through the passage verse by verse.

Daniel 12

> Daniel 12:11–13
> 11 And from the time that the regular burnt offering is taken
> away and the **abomination that makes desolate** is set up,
> there shall be 1,290 days. 12 Blessed is he who waits and
> arrives at the 1,335 days. 13 But go your way till the end.
> And you shall rest and shall stand in your allotted place at
> the end of the days."

Daniel 12 is the final section of the prophecies of Daniel. This section actually begins at Daniel 11:36 with the final "willful king" at the time of the end. Remember, chapter separations are not in the original text. So when Daniel 12:1 begins by saying, "At that time shall arise Michael," he is referring to the "time of the end" that he was just addressing a few verses earlier in 11:35, 40. It is one continuous flow of history.

So when exactly is this "time of the end"? Many Bible prophecy speculators assume it is the end of history when Jesus returns. But they would be seriously wrong. I do not have the space here to exegete every detail of this section, so I will stick to a few major points that argue against the context of our future and for the context of our past in the first-century days of ancient Rome and Titus Vespasian (if the reader wants more detail, see my podcast series, Daniel and End Times Prophecy).[13] Please keep in mind I am not arguing here that there is no

[13] https://www.youtube.com/playlist?list=PL5TyMLcYh4AOPA4WGoSAr9rSxUEMgv2hC

return of Christ in our future but simply arguing that Daniel is not talking about that event. He is talking about the first coming of Messiah at the end of the Gentile kingdoms.

The final kingdom of Daniel's four kingdoms. First, remember the context of Daniel's prophecies that we established earlier on. Daniel's prophecies are all about the four kingdoms that would rule over Israel until Messiah came: Babylon, Medo-Persia, Greece, and Rome. The vision of the large statue of four metals (Daniel 2), then the vision of the four great hybrid beasts from the sea (Daniel 7), and then the vision of the charging ram and the one-horned goat (Daniel 8) all reiterate those four kingdoms with differing focus. We read about Babylon in Daniel 1-7, then Medo-Persia in Daniel 8-11, which occurred during the lifetime of Daniel. Daniel 11-12 follows with predictions about the final two kingdoms of Greece and Rome. Messiah would come "in the days of these kings," specifically Rome, to usher in Messiah's new covenant kingdom (Daniel 2:44-45; 9:24-27).

Remember we have already seen that Daniel 11 chronicles with amazing precision the third kingdom, Greece, with its Syrian Wars of the third century BC, ending with the abomination of desolation by King Antiochus IV Epiphanes (11:21-35). So when Daniel begins to address the final king that "shall do as he wills" at "the time of the end" in 11:36-45, we are in the fourth and final kingdom of Rome. After all, what kingdom comes immediately after Greece in Daniel's prophetic timeline? Not some future symbolic or speculative rebuilt Roman kingdom thousands of years later but the real-world Rome that arose after Greece in real-world history. The big picture context of Daniel demands that the time of the end is during the ancient Roman kingdom (empire).

But isn't the time of the end the end of all time?

Time of the end. In Daniel 12, the divine messenger explains that the second abomination of desolation comes at the time of the end or the end of the days.

Daniel 12:9, 13
He said, "Go your way, Daniel, for the words are shut up and sealed until **the time of the end**.... But go your way **till the end**. And you shall rest and shall stand in your allotted place at **the end of the days**."

When they read those words, too many Christians impose their own preconceived cultural assumptions upon the phrase "time of the end," "end of the days," or "end time." They read them out of context. The primary rule of understanding the Bible in its ancient context is to let Scripture interpret Scripture. When we read the words "time of the end," we must not *assume* it means what we want it to mean, the end of all time or the end of the space-time universe. We must ask according to biblical precedent and context, "The end of what?" Let's let Daniel tell us exactly what he means by the end.

Daniel 8:19–23
19 He said, "Behold, I will make known to you what shall
be at **the latter end of the indignation ["curse"],** for it
refers to the appointed **time of the end**. 20 As for the ram
that you saw with the two horns, these are the kings of
Media and Persia. 21 And the goat is the king of Greece.
And the great horn between his eyes is the first king. 22 As
for the horn that was broken, in place of which four others
arose, four kingdoms shall arise from his nation, but not
with his power. 23 And at **the latter end of their kingdom, when the transgressors have reached their limit,** a king
of bold face, one who understands riddles, shall arise.

The time of the end is the "latter end of the indignation" or curse upon Israel when the transgressors have reached their limit. This occurs at the latter end of the four Greek "horn" kingdoms that came out of the horn of Alexander. Antiochus Epiphanes was at that latter end of those Greek kingdoms. In fact, it was during his reign that the Roman republic asserted her power over the Greek kingdoms of Seleucia and Ptolemies of Egypt. After the death of Antiochus Epiphanes, those Greek kingdoms began to crumble under Rome's ascendancy. Shortly thereafter in 65 BC under Julius Caesar, Rome would evolve into the Roman empire, the last of Daniel's four kingdoms.

Daniel 9:24-27 states that Messiah would finish the transgression of Israel, put an end to sin, atone for iniquity, and bring in his everlasting kingdom of righteousness. Israel's curse would be ended with the coming of Messiah. In context, Daniel was writing about the Messiah *ending* the transgression of Israel and *ending* sin with his atonement for iniquity at the cross (Daniel 9:24). And that was linked to *the end* of the holy city and temple (9:26). Daniel reiterates this *end* of the temple again in 12:11 with the second abomination of desolation. So "the end" in Daniel's prophecy is not the end of history or the end of time. It is the end of Israel's sin of idolatry against Yahweh through Messiah that would occur in the days of Rome at the end of the four kingdoms.

11:36-45 – the final "king that shall do as he wills … at the time of the end" is a ruler who is a part of that fourth and final kingdom. There are several strong options for who this Roman king was: Julius Caesar and the line of Caesars, the Roman general Titus, or King Herod the Great. I am not certain as to which of these three positions I am most persuaded. I find them each compelling. I would recommend further study.[14] But I lean toward King Herod, the Edomite king over Judea and client king of Rome. He certainly magnified himself above gods (Daniel 11:36). He was king when Messiah was born to end "the indignation" of Israel (11:36). As an Edomite, he paid no attention to the god of his

---

[14] Jay Rogers argues that it is the line of Caesars beginning with Julius: Jay Rogers, *In the Days of These Kings: The Book of Daniel in Preterist Perspective* (Clermont, FL: Media House International, 2017).

Duncan McKenzie makes a good argument that Titus is the king of Daniel 11:36: McKenzie PhD, Duncan W., *The Antichrist and the Second Coming: A Preterist Examination Volume I* (Kindle Locations 2896-2903). Xulon Press.

Philip Mauro argues for Herod the Great: Philip Mauro, *The Seventy Weeks and the Great Tribulation: A Study of the Last Two Visions of Daniel, and of the Olivet Discourse of the Lord Jesus Christ* (Public Domain, 1921, 1944),

James Jordan also makes a persuasive case that the "Little Horn" of Daniel 8:9-26 is also Herod the Great, rather than Antiochus Epiphanes. This would not change the overall interpretation or the other passages that still refer to Antiochus. See James B. Jordan, *The Handwriting on the Wall: A Commentary on the Book of Daniel* (Powder Springs, GA: American Vision, 2007), 424-437.

fathers, Abraham, Isaac, and Jacob (11:37). He built mighty fortresses as he rejected Yahweh (11:38-39). He divided his land for favors (11:39). The final section of this king's interaction with the kings of the south and north (11:40-45) reflects Herod's experience with Caesar Augustus (king of the north) and Egyptian queen Cleopatra (king of the south). The major actor "he" in that section is the king of the north, Augustus. The passage describes his victory over Antony and Cleopatra in the battle of Actium in 31 BC.[15]

As Bible commentator James Jordan explains:

> Why is attention given to these events, out of the many in Herod's reign? I believe it is because these events (a) fully established Rome's domination over the near east once and for all; (b) ended the separate history of the South, thus bringing to an end the Alexandrian history that began in Daniel 11:3; and (c) established Octavian Caesar, soon to take the name Augustus, as ruler of the Roman empire, thus setting the stage for the events described when Daniel's sealed book is reopened in the book of Revelation [in the first century].[16]

12:1-3 – "And many of those who sleep in the dust of the earth shall awake, some to everlasting life, and some to shame and everlasting contempt." This is a famous passage that many assume refers to the physical resurrection at the end of history and the return of Christ. But since it takes place in the days of ancient Rome, it is not in fact about the second coming. It is about the *first coming* of Christ. It wouldn't make sense for Daniel to completely skip over the most important hope of the Old Testament, the first coming of Messiah, to talk about a second coming out of context. This resurrection is simply Daniel's reiteration

---

[15] For a good narrative of this fulfillment see, Bruce Gore, *Historical and Chronological Context of the Bible* (Bruce Gore, 2006), Chapter 11, pages 15-16.

[16] James B. Jordan, *The Handwriting on the Wall: A Commentary on the Book of Daniel* (Powder Springs, GA: American Vision, 2007), 606–607.

of his contemporary Ezekiel's obvious metaphorical resurrection of Israel when Messiah comes (Ezekiel 37). Many Jews would rise from their spiritual death to everlasting life in Christ (through faith) while some of those Jews would spiritually rise to shame in rejecting Jesus and end in everlasting contempt. Jesus would be the spiritual Promised Land of Israel unto which they would be regathered (Hebrews 9:15; 118-16; 12:22-24).[17]

12:7 – "[the length of time for these predictions to take place] would be for a time, times, and half a time…"

A time, times, and half a time is another way of saying 3 1/2. "Titus's campaign of destruction against the Jews lasted exactly three-and-a-half years (March/April AD 67 to August/September AD 70) and resulted in the destruction of the Jewish nation."[18]

12:7 – "…and that when the shattering of the power of the holy people comes to an end all these things would be finished."

The "power of the holy people" in the Bible is the covenant. The shattering of that power or covenant was the end of the old covenant that was historically and publicly ended in AD 70 with the destruction of the incarnation of that old covenant system, the holy temple (Matthew 21:38-44, fulfilling Joshua 23:16; Galatians 4:24-31).

12:9 – "He said, "Go your way, Daniel, for the words are shut up and sealed until the time of the end."

12:13 – "But go your way till the end. And you shall rest and shall stand in your allotted place at the end of the days."

The "time of the end" is not "the end of time." "End of the days" does not mean "end of all days" but merely the end of the days for these

---

[17] For a detailed explanation of how Jesus Christ fulfills the Land Promise see my book, Brian Godawa, Israel in Bible Prophecy: The New Testament Fulfillment of the Promise to Abraham (Warrior Poet Publishing, 2021), 22-32.

[18] McKenzie PhD, Duncan W., *The Antichrist and the Second Coming: A Preterist Examination Volume* I (Xulon Press. Kindle Edition).

prophecies of the four Gentile kingdoms (12:12). Those days were ended with the AD 70 destruction of the temple in Jerusalem.

12:11-12 – "And from the time that the regular burnt offering is taken away and the abomination that makes desolate is set up, there shall be 1,290 days. Blessed is he who waits and arrives at the 1,335 days."

The Hebrew grammar underlying this verse is unclear as to whether the taking away of the burnt offering is first, the arrival of the abomination of desolation is first, or whether the two incidents are to be considered together as the starting point for the days.

The ancient Jewish historian Josephus indicates the exact date in AD 70 when the daily sacrifices had stopped during the war with Rome.

> Josephus *Wars of the Jews*, 6.2.1 (93)
> And now Titus gave orders to his soldiers that were with him to dig up the foundations of the tower of Antonia, and make him a ready passage for his army to come [into the Jerusalem temple] … on that very day, which was the seventeenth day of Panemus [Tamuz], the sacrifice called "the Daily Sacrifice" had failed, and had not been offered to God.[19]

Based on this interpretation of the ending of the sacrifice in AD 70, Bible scholar Philip Mauro concluded:

> The first approach of the Roman armies under Cestius is described by Josephus in his book of Wars, II 17, 10. This was in the month corresponding to our November, A.D. 66. The taking away of the daily sacrifice was in the month Panemus, corresponding to the Hebrew Tammuz, and our July, A.D. 70. Thus the measure of time between the two

[19] Flavius Josephus and William Whiston, *The Works of Josephus: Complete and Unabridged* (Peabody: Hendrickson, 1987), 731.

events was three years, and part of a fourth [or 1,290 days].[20]

Those Roman armies that were previously under Cestius would return 3 1/2 years later led personally by the co-emperor Titus. When Titus captured the holy city and temple, it was the end of the siege but not the end of the war atrocities that would commence upon victory. The additional 45 days that resulted in Daniel's blessing to those surviving 1,335 days is a reference to those few Jews who had been able to hide or escape the pillage and plunder of the Roman forces in the city.

To conclude, let's look at the whole of the Daniel prophecy again with my notations to see how it all flows.

> Daniel 9:24–27 (NASB95)
> [24] Seventy weeks [of years or 490 years] have been decreed for your people [Israel] and your holy city [Jerusalem], to finish the transgression [of Israel's spiritual idolatry], to make an end of sin, to make atonement for iniquity [through the cross], to bring in everlasting righteousness [with the gospel], to seal up vision and prophecy [that have all been pointing to Jesus] and to anoint the most holy place [Jesus].
> [25] "So you are to know and discern that from the issuing of a decree to restore and rebuild Jerusalem [by Artaxerxes in 457-8 BC] until Messiah the Prince [Jesus] there will be seven weeks [49 years] and sixty-two weeks [+434 years = 483 years]; it will be built again, with plaza and moat, even in times of distress [in the days of Nehemiah].
> [26] Then after the sixty-two weeks [after 483 years around AD 30-32] the Messiah will be cut off [from the Father on the cross for us by taking on our sin] and have nothing, and the people [Roman soldiers] of the prince who is to come [Jesus as sovereign God using them] will destroy the city

---

[20] Mauro, Philip. *The Seventy Weeks and the Great Tribulation* (K-Locations 2288-2319). K-Edition.

> [Jerusalem] and the sanctuary [the temple]. And its end will come with a flood [in AD 70]; even to the end there will be war; desolations are determined [as Jesus predicted and Josephus described in *The Wars of the Jews*].
> 27 And he [Messiah Jesus] will make a firm [new] covenant with the many [remnant believers] for one week [the kingdom preached in AD 30], but in the middle of the week [AD 33] he [Jesus] will put a stop to sacrifice and grain offering [by his once for all sacrifice on the cross]; and [within 40 years] on the wing of abominations will come one [Titus the Roman general] who makes desolate [the temple], even until a complete destruction [in AD 70], one that is decreed, is poured out on the desolate.

Because of their preconceived eschatology, most futurists separate the abomination of desolation from the coming of Messiah. They think that the Seventy Weeks prophecy is talking about the first coming of Jesus, then jumps ahead thousands of years into the future to talk about an Antichrist who is the abomination of desolation. They have to impose an imagined third rebuilt temple and destruction and ignore the second rebuilt temple and destruction spoken of in the text. They have to stick a 2,000-year gap into the prophecy, which simply isn't there. It's not even hinted at. They must add to the Word of God to keep their system working. In reality, the context consistently fits the first century where all those things occurred.

And if you don't believe me, let's ask Jesus.

Jesus and the Abomination of Desolation

It is well known that Jesus spoke of the coming "abomination of desolation spoken of by the prophet Daniel" (Matthew 24:15). When futurist prophecy speculators read his statement that took place on the Mount of Olives, they see it as the Antichrist, the Beast, some demonic person in our own future who has yet to appear and set foot in the temple in Jerusalem (which is supposedly yet to be rebuilt). This is alleged to happen in the midst of a "great tribulation" in our future and heralds a betrayal of a treaty made between the Antichrist and Israel. Unfortunately, none of this imagined futuristic science fiction is in the passage, let alone in the entire Bible. Let's take a look at Jesus's words in biblical context.

> Matthew 24:15–20
> [Jesus:] "So when you see the **abomination of desolation**
> spoken of by the prophet Daniel, standing in the holy place
> (let the reader understand), 16 then let those who are in
> Judea flee to the mountains. 17 Let the one who is on the
> housetop not go down to take what is in his house, 18 and
> let the one who is in the field not turn back to take his
> cloak. 19 And alas for women who are pregnant and for
> those who are nursing infants in those days! 20 Pray that
> your flight may not be in winter or on a Sabbath.

This Generation

So many Christians come to this passage with a preconceived assumption that it is in our future when the actual context of the prophecy through Jesus's own words says it already happened in our past to his generation.

Jesus himself tells us the interpretive key to the abomination of desolation in several ways. First and most important is that the entire prophecy of events to happen in Matthew 24, including the abomination of desolation," is bookended by a repeated phrase: *this generation.*

> Matthew 23:36
> Truly, I say to you, all these things will come upon **this generation.**

> Matthew 24:34
> Truly, I say to you, **this generation** will not pass away until all these things take place.

So Jesus tells us that all these things he was predicting—the destruction of the temple, wars and rumors of wars, persecution, apostasy, the abomination of desolation—were to come upon his generation that was rejecting him. In fact, most of them would not pass away until it occurred (Matthew 16:28).

Like the 40-year wilderness generation that was judged for their unbelief, so Jesus's generation would be judged for their unbelief. Their rejection of Messiah is exactly what Jesus was explaining in Matthew 23.

> Matthew 23:36–24:2
> "Truly, I say to you, all these things will come upon **this generation**. O Jerusalem, Jerusalem, the city that kills the prophets and stones those who are sent to it! … See, **your house [the temple] is left to you desolate**." … Jesus left the temple and was going away, when his disciples came to point out to him the buildings of the temple. But he answered them, "You see all these, do you not? Truly, I say to you, **there will not be left here one stone upon another that will not be thrown down**."

A generation was about 40 years, another symbolic number. And it just so happens that the second temple was destroyed about 40 years later in AD 70 before Jesus's generation had passed away.

There have been attempts to try to spin away the plain meaning of the phrase "this generation" to mean anything other than the generation to whom Jesus was speaking. All of them fall flat in the face of the explicit definition given by Matthew and all the New Testament. Everywhere Matthew uses the phrase "this generation," it is a reference *to the contemporary generation of Jesus*, the ones to whom he was speaking. Not only that, but it was also most often used as a derogatory term of judgment upon those who were rejecting Jesus as Messiah.[21]

---

[21] See also: Matthew 12:39–42 (Luk e11:29-32); 12:41, 45; 11:16-19; 17:17; Mark 8:38; 9:19; Luke 9:41; 17:25; Philippians 2:15; Acts 2:40; 1 Thessalonians 2:14-16.

> Matthew 12:41
> The men of Nineveh will rise up at the judgment with **this generation** and condemn it, for they repented at the preaching of Jonah, and behold, something greater than Jonah is here.
>
> Luke 17:25
> But first he must suffer many things and be rejected by **this generation**.
>
> Luke 11:50–51
> So that the blood of all the prophets, shed from the foundation of the world, may be **charged against this generation**.... Yes, I tell you, it will be required of **this generation**.

So when Jesus predicts the destruction of the temple in Matthew 23:37-24:2 as judgment upon the first-century Jews for rejecting Messiah and states that everything included with that judgment would occur to "this generation," he is referencing his generation to whom he was speaking. When Jesus uses the personal second person accusative "you" over 35 times—"when *you* see," "when such and such happens to *you*"—directly to his audience, it is safe to say that he meant the generation to whom he was speaking, not some future generation of people that have nothing to do with Jesus.

Imagine being a person listening to Jesus telling you that when you see these things and when these things happen to you, then you should know that destruction is near. Then you discover that he wasn't talking to you at all but was speaking to and about a future generation of people thousands of years from your generation. You could fairly accuse Jesus of misleading his entire audience. Of course, I do not believe Jesus would ever mislead or lie. My point is that the claim that Jesus was not speaking to his audience but to an imaginary future one is tantamount to such misinformation.

In my novel series Chronicles of the Apocalypse, I tell the story of the destruction of Jerusalem and the temple in AD 70 by the Roman forces of Titus. I based it on the only existing full manuscript detailing the infamous event by one of its own participants, Jewish historian Flavius Josephus. His narrative reads like a virtual point-by-point fulfillment of Jesus's prophecy in Matthew 24.

Here are a couple paragraphs from Josephus's account of the AD 70 destruction of Jerusalem and its temple where he claims fulfillment of Daniel's two abominations of desolation as referencing successively Antiochus Epiphanes and Rome under Titus. Josephus also considered the Romans as God's means of judgment. If Josephus wasn't a Jew who most definitely didn't accept Jesus as Messiah, you would think he was a Christian quoting Jesus.

> Flavius Josephus, *Antiquities* 10.276
> And indeed it so came to pass, that our nation suffered these things under Antiochus Epiphanes, according to Daniel's vision, and what he wrote many years before they came to pass. In the very same manner **Daniel also wrote concerning the Roman government, and that our country should be made desolate by them**.

> Flavius Josephus, *The Wars of the Jews* 6.2.1 §110
> And are not both the city and the entire temple now full of the dead bodies of your countrymen? It is God therefore, **it is God himself who is bringing on this fire, to purge that city and temple by means of the Romans**, and is going to pluck up this city, which is full of your **pollutions**.

Flee to the Mountains

Another element of context to the abomination of desolation passage that reinforces a first-century fulfillment is the advice Jesus gives to his audience to flee Judea when they see the abomination of desolation at the gates.

> Matthew 24:17-20
> Then let those who are in Judea flee to the mountains. Let the one who is on the housetop not go down to take what is in his house, and let the one who is in the field not turn back to take his cloak. And alas for women who are pregnant and for those who are nursing infants in those days! Pray that your flight may not be in winter or on a Sabbath.

None of this could apply to the present-day thousands of years after Christ. Fleeing to the mountains today would be meaningless in the face of modern travel and war technology. Winter, Sabbath, and pregnancy would not be problematic for modern travelers. Back in the first century, the mountains surrounding Israel were actual places of refuge from the war that had spread throughout the land. But it would be difficult to flee there carrying small children, ferrying household goods in carts or wagons, or even just for the elderly, incapacitated, or heavily pregnant.

Jesus was telling his followers how to escape the judgment that was coming upon Jerusalem and Israel for rejecting Messiah. And escape they did. Early church historian Eusebius recorded how the Christians followed Jesus' warnings.

> Eusebius, *Ecclesiastical History* 3:5
> But the people of the church in Jerusalem had been commanded by a revelation, vouchsafed to approved men there before the war, to leave the city and to dwell in a certain town of Perea called Pella. And when those that believed in Christ had come thither from Jerusalem, then, as if the royal city of the Jews and the whole land of Judea were entirely destitute of holy men, the judgment of God at length overtook those who had committed such outrages against Christ and his apostles, and totally destroyed that generation of impious men.[22]

---

[22] Eusebius of Caesaria, "The Church History of Eusebius," in *Eusebius: Church History, Life of Constantine the Great, and Oration in Praise of Constantine*, ed. Philip Schaff and Henry Wace, trans. Arthur Cushman McGiffert, vol.

My second book in the *Chronicles of the Apocalypse* series, Remnant: Rescue of the Elect tells this story in dramatic fiction. The Christians were spared from God's judgment because they were no longer part of the old system, the old age of the old covenant. They had both figuratively and literally fled all of it. God was destroying the temple as the incarnation of that old covenant.

Since most Jews did not embrace the new covenant, they were in a dead religion. The Roman army was like vultures gathering around the carcass of that dead religion to finish it off just as Jesus stated in this same Olivet discourse.

> Matthew 24:28
> Wherever the corpse is, there the vultures will gather.

But there is even more hermeneutical help that Jesus gives us in interpreting his words. More precisely, Luke gives us a literal explanation of what the "abomination of desolation" actually was in his generation.

Surrounded by Pagan Armies

Let's take a step back for more context. Matthew uses the Hebrew term abomination of desolation. This is important because the book of Matthew was written to Jews. It has many Hebraisms and Old Testament references and concepts that most Jews would know when reading them.

The gospel of Luke was written more for a Gentile audience, so he tended to explain things or translate them for the non-Hebrew. The abomination of desolation is one of those things Luke translated for us.

Luke 21 and Mark 13 both contain the same sermon also found in Matthew 24. But there are some variations in the text. Let me put them side by side so you can see the obvious correlation.

1, *A Select Library of the Nicene and Post-Nicene Fathers of the Christian Church, Second Series* (New York: Christian Literature Company, 1890), 138.

Matthew 24:15–16 "So **when you see the abomination of desolation** spoken of by the prophet Daniel, standing in the holy place (let the reader understand), then let those who are in Judea flee to the mountains."	Luke 21:20–22 "But **when you see Jerusalem surrounded by armies**, then know that its desolation has come near … Then let those who are in Judea flee to the mountains."	Mark 13:14 (NASB95) "But **when you see the abomination of desolation standing where it should not be** (let the reader understand), then those who are in Judea must flee to the mountains."

The Hebrew image of "abomination of desolation" in Matthew and Mark is translated by Luke to be "Jerusalem surrounded by armies." So Luke makes clear that the correct interpretation intended by Jesus of "abomination of desolation" is *Jerusalem being surrounded by armies.* Specifically, pagan idolatrous armies.

Did this happen in the first century as we have been arguing? Why, yes, it did. In A.D. 66, the abominable Roman armies did in fact surround Jerusalem just as Jesus had foretold. In this sense, they were "standing in a holy place" around the holy city "where it [the pagan army] should not be." Like Antiochus Epiphanes and his Greek armies setting up their idol of Zeus, so a general of Titus named Cestius with his Roman legions surrounded Jerusalem with their idolatrous standards of Caesar, the abomination of desolation (images of desolation). Providentially, Josephus tells us that for some unknown reason, Cestius stopped short of attacking the temple and just left with all his army. This allowed the Christians of the city the opportunity to flee to the mountains.

A couple years later, Titus returned with that army and finished what was started by conquering the city of Jerusalem and capturing the temple. While there, he set up Rome's idolatrous standards of Caesar in the temple as an abomination of desolation. Jewish historian Josephus described the event.

> And now the Romans … upon burning of the holy house itself, and of all the buildings round about it, brought their

> ensigns to the temple ... and there did they offer sacrifices to them, and there did they make Titus imperator, with the greatest acclamations of joy.[23]

It could not be more clear. Pagan rulers and their armies are abominable defilers of sacred space.

The destruction of the city and temple were a main focus of the prophetic near-future for Jesus and the apostles. In fact, Jesus referred on another occasion to the destruction of the city of Jerusalem as punishment for the Jews not recognizing the time of the visitation of God in Messiah.

> Luke 19:41–44
> And when he drew near and saw the city [Jerusalem], he wept over it, saying, "Would that you, even you, had known on this day the things that make for peace! But now they are hidden from your eyes. For the days will come upon you, when your enemies will set up a barricade around you and surround you and hem you in on every side and tear you down to the ground, you and your children within you. And they will not leave one stone upon another in you, because you did not know the time of your visitation."

Remember the language that Jesus used in Matthew 24 about God not leaving one stone of the temple upon another? Well, he used it here again, linking those two prophecies about the destruction that was coming in AD 70. At that time, Titus had his army set up a barricade all around Jerusalem, just as Jesus said they would. And just as Jesus had

---

[23] Flavius Josephus, *The Wars of the Jews* 6.6.1, §316. Josephus also describes the standards as considered idolatrous by the Jews in *The Wars of the Jews* 2.9.2 §169-170 "Now Pilate, who was sent as procurator into Judea by Tiberius, sent by night those images of Caesar that are called Ensigns, into Jerusalem. (170) This excited a very great tumult among the Jews when it was day; for those that were near them were astonished at the sight of them, as indications that their laws were trodden underfoot: for those laws do not permit any sort of image to be brought into the city." Flavius Josephus and William Whiston, *The Works of Josephus: Complete and Unabridged* (Peabody: Hendrickson, 1987), 608.

prophesied, they subsequently tore down both city and temple to the ground, not leaving one stone of that temple upon another.

Once again, Jesus makes clear that the reason for this judgment of destruction upon the city and temple was because its Jewish residents "did not know the time of your visitation" (v 44). That visitation was the visitation of God himself incarnate in the Messiah (Luke 1:68; 7:16). This first-century judgment for rejecting Messiah turns out to be a major motif of Jesus's own ministry (Matthew 11:16-18; 12:39-42; 21:33-45; 23:29-39; Mark 8:38-9:1).

The abomination that brought desolation to Jerusalem and the temple is not a prophecy of our future but a fulfillment in our past. It was the Roman ruler Titus Vespasian and his pagan armies who would defile the holy place and destroy both temple and holy city in AD 70, thereby fulfilling Daniel's prophecy.

> Daniel 9:26–27
> And the people of the prince who is to come shall destroy the city and the sanctuary. Its end shall come with a flood, and to the end there shall be war. Desolations are decreed.… And on the wing of abominations shall come one who makes desolate, until the decreed end is poured out on the desolate.

I am very aware that applying the abomination of desolation in Daniel 12 to Titus in AD 70 will offend some futuristic prophecy schemes and scenarios. As I have already indicated, there are many questions to be answered about the rest of Daniel's prophecies, but this booklet is a vanguard for addressing those issues by starting with the immediate context around the abomination of desolation before working outward to the rest of the story. The reader can pursue a fuller treatment in my teaching videos called Daniel and End Times Prophecy.

What About the Image of the Beast?

Another question may arise in the mind of the Christian who has a futurist orientation in their prophecy system. What about Revelation 13? That passage talks about the Land Beast creating an image of the Sea Beast for the people to worship. Isn't that the abomination of desolation that Jesus was talking about?

> Revelation 13:14–15
> [The land beast told the people] to make an image for the [sea] beast that was wounded by the sword and yet lived. And it was allowed to give breath to the image of the beast, so that the image of the beast might even speak and might cause those who would not worship the image of the beast to be slain.

Though this passage is certainly about idolatrous worship of an image, there is no connection to the abomination in Daniel or Jesus. First, the words abomination and desolation are nowhere mentioned or even hinted at. This is a minimum requirement if one is to make a connection to such a particular prophecy.

Second, this beastly image is not said to have any relation to the Jerusalem temple whatsoever, which is a key part of the definition of the biblical abomination of desolation. Some believe this image is placed in the temple, but that is an assumption simply not in the text. This is commonly called eisegesis when a person imposes their own extrabiblical system upon the text in order to keep their system from falling apart.

Third, the existence of an idolatrous image in a text does not automatically connect it to the abomination of desolation predicted by Daniel or Jesus. There are multiple places in the Old Testament where abominable images of Asherah and other Canaanite deities are spoken of being in the temple (2 Kings 21:4-7; 23:6). Any time an idol is brought into God's house, it could be accused of being an abomination. Though one could fairly call them abominations of desolation *by way of analogy*, one could never call them *the* abomination of desolation spoken of by Daniel and Jesus.

Of course, addressing Revelation further takes us far afield of the purpose of this examination. Many believe Revelation to be a prophecy about our future. But see my podcast series Revelation & End Times Bible Prophecy[24] for a detailed exegesis of Revelation as a prophecy about the first-century judgment of Jesus Christ upon Jerusalem and the temple with the coming of the new covenant kingdom of God. Or read my novel series Chronicles of the Apocalypse for the narrative telling of that story in the first century: the origin of the book of Revelation. Shocking to those who have been taught a futurist paradigm as if it were the only orthodox option. Shocking but more biblical.

•••••

If you liked this book, then please help me out by writing a positive review of it on Amazon. That is one of the best ways to say thank you to me as an author. It really does help my sales and status. Thanks!—*Brian Godawa*

More Books by Brian Godawa

See www.Godawa.com for more information on other books by Brian Godawa. Check out his other series below.

Chronicles of the Nephilim

Chronicles of the Nephilim is a saga that charts the rise and fall of the Nephilim giants of Genesis 6 and their place in the evil plans of the fallen angelic Sons of God called "The Watchers." The story starts in the days of Enoch and continues on through the Bible until the arrival of the Messiah, Jesus. The prelude to Chronicles of the Apocalypse. ChroniclesOfTheNephilim.com. (affiliate link)

---

24 https://www.youtube.com/playlist?list=PL5TyMLcYh4AOz1_nbyeMQCQWW7pk097sG

Chronicles of the Apocalypse

Chronicles of the Apocalypse is an origin story of the most controversial book of the Bible: Revelation. A historical conspiracy thriller series in first century Rome set against the backdrop of explosive spiritual warfare of Satan and his demonic Watchers. ChroniclesOfTheApocalypse.com. (affiliate link)

Chronicles of the Watchers

Chronicles of the Watchers is a series that charts the influence of spiritual principalities and powers over the course of human history. The kingdoms of man in service to the gods of the nations at war. Completely based on ancient historical and mythological research. ChroniclesOfTheWatchers.com. (affiliate link)

Great Offers By Brian Godawa

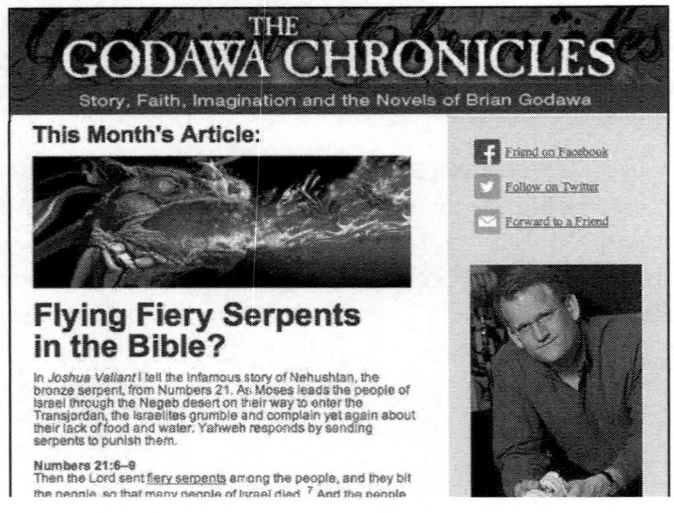

Get More Biblical Imagination

Sign up Online For The Godawa Chronicles

www.Godawa.com

Updates and Freebies
of the Books of Brian Godawa
Special Discounts, Weird Bible Facts!

About the Author

Brian Godawa is a respected Christian writer and best-selling author of novels and biblical theology. His supernatural Bible epic novels combine creative imagination with orthodox Christian theology in a way that transcends both entertainment and preachiness.

His love for Jesus and storytelling was forged in the crucible of worldview apologetics and Hollywood screenwriting, as he began a career in movies and eventually expanded into the world of novels.

His first novel series, *Chronicles of the Nephilim* has been in the Top 10 of Biblical Fiction on Amazon for more than a decade, selling over 350,000 books. His popular book *Hollywood Worldviews: Watching Films with Wisdom and Discernment* is used as a textbook in Christian film schools around the country. His movies *To End All Wars* and *Alleged* have won multiple movie awards such as Cannes Film Festival and the Heartland International Film Festival.

He lives in Texas with the most amazing wife a man could ever pray for and is accountable to a local church. He reads too many books and watches too many movies. He knows, he knows, he should get out more.

Find out more about his blog and his other books, lectures, and online courses for sale at his website, **www.godawa.com.**

BLANK PAGE

BLANK PAGE

BLANK PAGE

BLANK PAGE

BLANK PAGE

BLANK PAGE

BLANK PAGE

BLANK PAGE

BLANK PAGE

Made in the USA
Coppell, TX
13 December 2024